Never Mind the Bagpipes

A Piper's Tale
by
Allan Jardine

Published by New Generation Publishing in 2021

Copyright © Allan Jardine 2021
© All illustrations copyright Allan Jardine

First Edition

The author asserts the moral right under the Copyright, Designs and Patents Act 1988 to be identified as the author of this work.

All Rights reserved. No part of this publication may be reproduced, stored in a retrieval system or transmitted, in any form or by any means without the prior consent of the author, nor be otherwise circulated in any form of binding or cover other than that which it is published and without a similar condition being imposed on the subsequent purchaser.

ISBN: 978-1-80031-181-7

www.newgeneration-publishing.com

New Generation Publishing

For my father

"Oh soldier lie doon in yer wee bed of straw
It's no very big and it's no very braw
But what wid ye dae if ye had nane at all
So soldier lie doon in yer wee bed of straw."

Robert Kirk

Never mind the Bagpipes

Introduction xi

Chapter 1. The Chanter 1

Chapter 2. The Box 9

Chapter 3. The Two Tables 19

Chapter 4. The Hogmanay Incident 29

Chapter 5. Air pistols at dawn. 39

Chapter 6. Smoke on the water............................ 51

Chapter 7. Tossers and soggy banners 61

Chapter 8. Hotel California 71

Chapter 9. No man is an island 81

Chapter 10. The Water of Life 89

Chapter 11. The Black Death 99

Chapter 13. A stitch in time 119

Epilogue 131

Appendix 1 133

Appendix 2 136

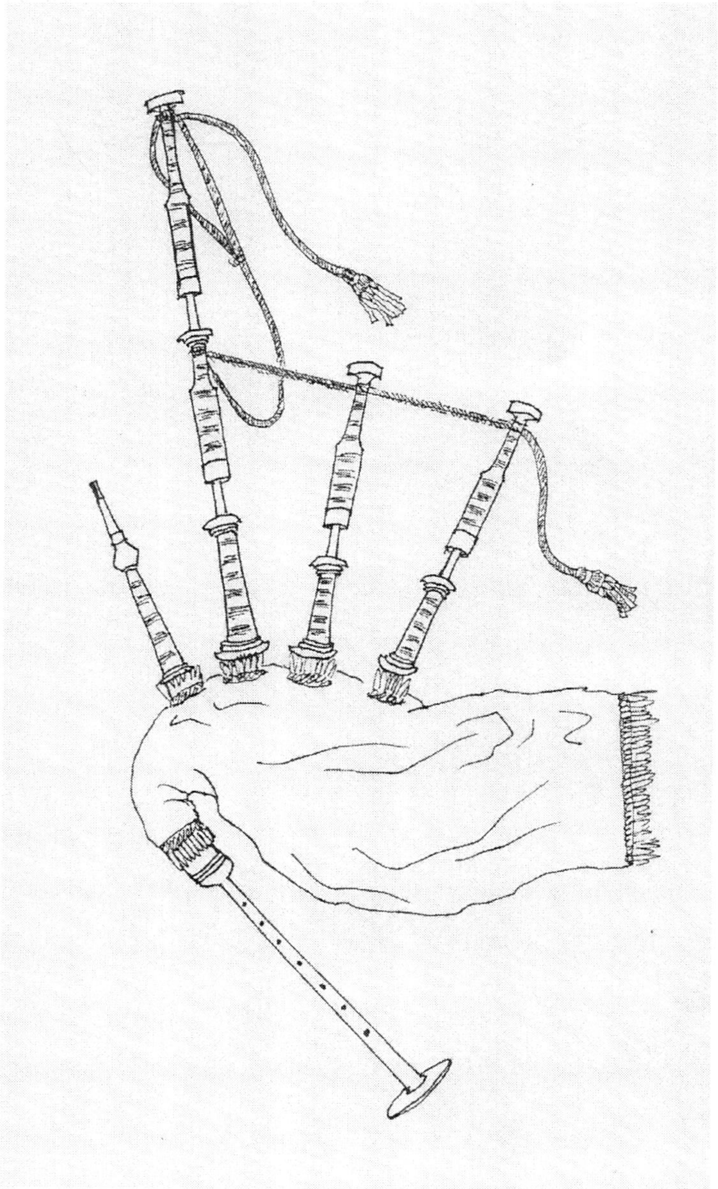

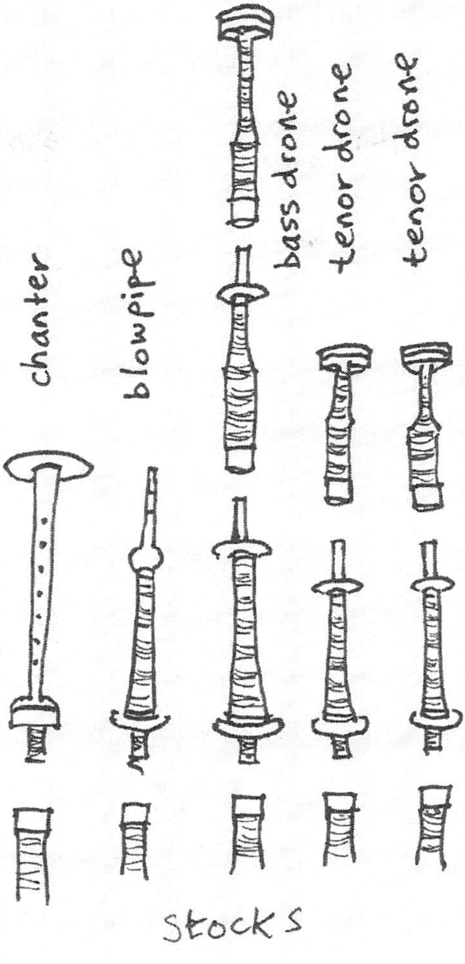
chanter
blowpipe
bass drone
tenor drone
tenor drone
stocks

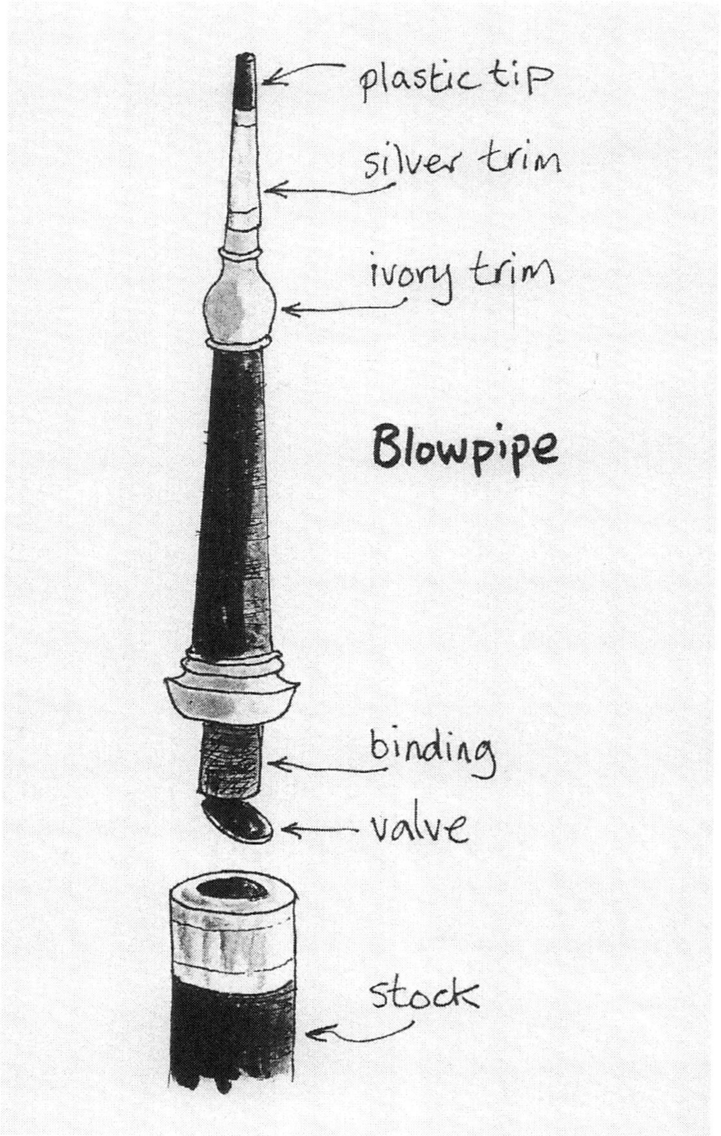
plastic tip
silver trim
ivory trim
Blowpipe
binding
valve
stock

A note

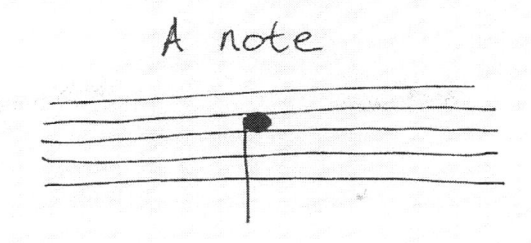

Two notes with grace note

Don't even think about it!

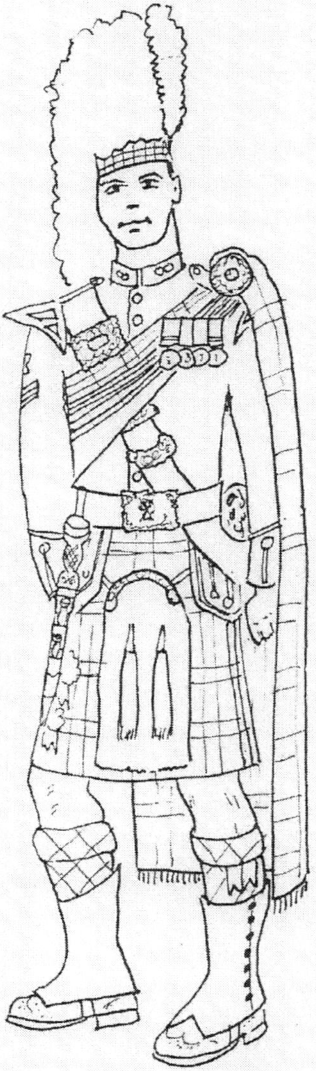

Introduction

This book is about the great Highland Bagpipes and not about me, although I do crop up an awful lot.It was not intended to be an autobiography, but I thought the best way to explain the instrument and related Scottish culture, was from my own experiences of them in chronological order. The project began after a profound session in The Jinglin' Geordie pub in Edinburgh, where my friend the artist Philip Braham suggested that I put down in print all the stories that I been recounting to the enthralled audience at the bar, so that's what I did. It is not a technical book, so I hope the old guard are not going to complain if a tunic button in one of my cartoons is upside down, or that I've spelt taorluath the wrong way. It's a humorous book and should be accepted as such. The events depicted here are all true, and every effort has been made to contact those persons involved, apart from Steve and John from Chicago, and if they're reading this, thanks for all the Johnny Walker Red Label in the Jolly Roger, Fort Lauderdale.

Allan Jardine, Edinburgh, March 2021

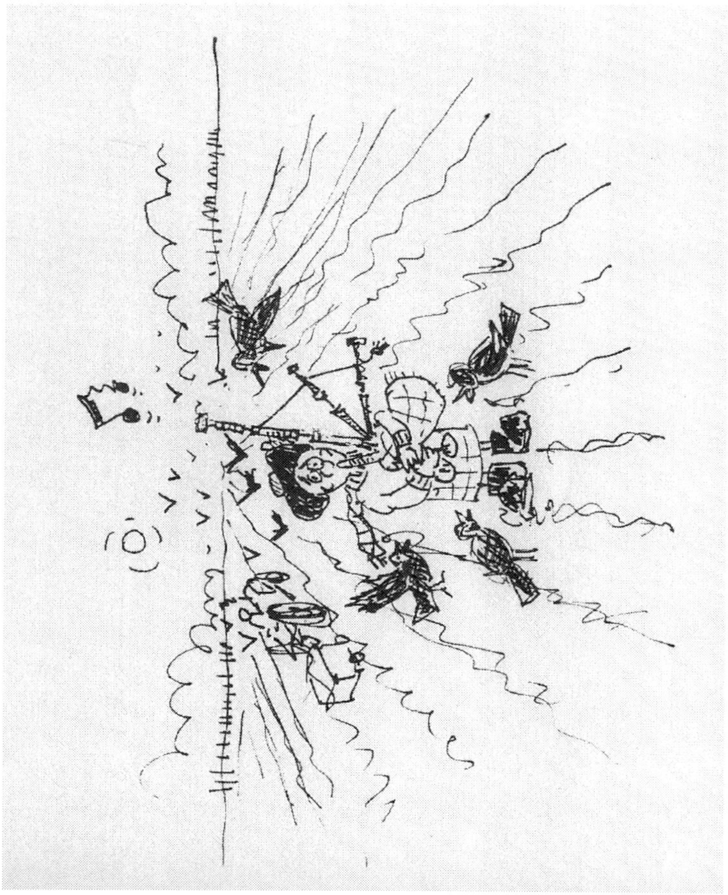

Chapter 1. The Chanter

"Rejoice O young man, in thy youth."
Ecclesiastes

I did not always want to be a Piper. In fact, when my father casually asked me one day, in passing almost, if I, perhaps, might want to learn the instrument, I categorically said no. Absolutely not. I was quite emphatic about it and thought that would be the end of the matter. I mean, why on earth would I? All that shortbread tin imagery sprang into my mind, of big men with hairy knees swathed in tartan, buckles in odd places and silly hats with feathers, puffing away for prancing girls pirouetting in their pumps at a Highland Games, or providing the sprightly soundtrack for young men and women mincing around a set of crossed Claymore swords waving their hands in the air, at a Ceilidh. Think of the poor Piper stood stoically outside the church at a wedding, in the rain, all dressed up and wailing away to the obvious disinterest of the guests or the happy couple, wrestling with an instrument that looks, in all honesty, somewhat ridiculous, and sounds, well, sounds the way it does.

So when I was leaving the gates of my primary school a few days later, and I was hailed by a teacher to come back in, I was immediately curious and suspicious in equal measure. I was informed, to my dismay and the teacher's glee, that I had been enrolled in bagpiping classes. These would take place on Tuesday and Thursday evenings after normal lessons, and that I would need to bring along something called a chanter. And that, it would appear, was that.

Before we go any further, we should really examine the history of the Bagpipes, but, and I'm sure you'll be glad to hear, that there isn't really any, so we won't. It's not that kind of book anyway. Suffice to say that records show instruments of a similar construction appearing all over the world at various times, so no one can really claim to have 'invented' the bag/pipe combination. No doubt the truth may be that long ago some master flute player's slave saw some children kicking about an inflated yak's bladder as a sort of prehistoric football, and had the bright idea of attaching something similar to the flute as a back- up air supply to supplement his master's lungs, and so allow continual playing. Quite possibly he also received a clip round the ear for making such a preposterous suggestion, but the seeds that were to grow into the modern instrument were sown. We do know that the bagpipes became popular in Scotland as a peasant instrument, with a sound designed to carry across the free open air of the glens, but unlike harps, lutes, violas and the like which were played in Court, nothing was ever documented about them, hence the lack of 'history'.

So it came to pass, one fine day back in 1970 when I was seven years old, a big road trip is being planned to visit Edinburgh to purchase this mysterious object called a Practice Chanter. We lived in the sleepy coastal village of Elie, in the county of Fife, Scotland, where Dad was a local dairy farmer in nearby Colinsburgh. Mum was a typical housewife of the period, quietly tidying up after the family and getting dinner ready for myself, my younger brother and my dad, as he kicked half a field of earth off his boots against the back door step.

We lived a fairly simple, rustic but happy life, in a time warp of self-sufficiency and bartering. I have fond memories of being sent out to the back garden to dig up some "tatties, some onions and a couple of carrots" for the accompaniment of the mince, in the bucketing rain, or of the shock of finding an alarming, wriggling, sack of live crabs on the doorstep with the morning milk bottles. Payment, apparently, for Dad having pulled some fisherman's boat out of the harbour with a tractor, before a storm.

A jaunt to the Big City was a major deal back then for us country folk, even if it was only an hour's drive away. It was usually a once a year event, like Christmas, and as such the necessary plans and preparations had to be made. The car would be washed, tyre and oil pressure checked and so on. Kilts would be laid out, pressed, and the silver on the sporran polished. I was fascinated by Dad's *Sgian Dubh*, a real dagger, by God, which I would go on to inherit later in life, and which would accompany me on many an adventure of a piping and general kilt wearing nonsense. On my first day at primary school I was made to wear a kilt, and boy, I wish I had that dagger down my sock when the teasing started.

Anyway, with Mum's 'to buy' list completed, the petrol tank full, and a grand waving off from the other villagers, it was with a giant whoosh that our big car was off to the capital. I always wondered why they dragged me along. I would get car sick but refrain from throwing up until ensconced in the restaurant at lunchtime. Never let it be said that the Jardine's were not sophisticated, so we would usually opt for a Chinese restaurant, ordering chow mien knowledgeably, although we were afraid to try anything else. Then the kitchen smells would just set me off. Usually all over Dad. I would try to reason with him that it was cheaper to have his kilt dry-cleaned again, than to have the car valeted, but I reckon it was the embarrassment that did it for him. The smell made people stare.

Dad and I would stand grumpily outside every department store on Princes Street, in our matching Jardine tartan kilts. Dad would puff manfully on his pipe, stroking his big handlebar moustache, with me pathetically resigned beside him, the men of the household letting the womenfolk do their thing inside. We even got our photos in *The Scotsman* newspaper once. It was around the Edinburgh Festival time so maybe they thought we were a novelty act of some sort. I remember the summer heat was unbearable in our tweed jackets and woollen tartan ties, but we braved it out like the soldiers we were. Decorum dictated that parasols would look, well, a bit girly, and that brings to mind that greatest of Scottish paradoxes, that the most feminine of clothing, a skirt, should be worn by the most manly of men, the Scotsman, but more of that later.

So, after stocking up on 'stuff' like sheets and towels, the odd kettle, new pyjamas for Dad, although he insisted he didn't need any - (maybe the cheque book was wearing thin by this time), oh, and a wee something here and there that had caught Mum's eye in the fashion department, it was off to that veritable emporium of all things Bagpipe – J & R Glen, of Edinburgh. Situated on the historic Lawnmarket, down the hill from Edinburgh Castle, it was a sort of cross between a Victorian cabinetmakers and Ollivander's wand shop in Diagon Alley. It had all the cheerfulness of a funeral parlour and made you feel like you were in a place that had, very recently, been visited by an extremely angry Tasmanian Devil.

A young man introduced us to a very old man called Young Mr Glen, who had seemingly been there all the time. He had become so at one with his shop that he startled us all when he moved, and gave off a faint whiff of mothballs. He began unnervingly eyeing me up with great intensity, and murmuring words in Dad's ear. My dad was by now gazing down from above with great solemnity and pride. After all, this was his son and heir being measured for his first chanter.

A practice chanter is not unlike a recorder, with which most people will be familiar, in that you blow air in one end, and by lifting fingers off holes in the tube, produce musical notes. Unlike a recorder, which has a slot cut in it to produce the sound, a chanter has a reed inside consisting of two thin pieces of cane, or more commonly plastic, bound together at one end. When air is passed through, the two free ends vibrate and produce sound. By placing the thumb of the left hand on the single back hole at the top end of the finger board, and the first three fingers of the same hand on the first three holes, you cover the top part, and the four fingers of the right hand cover the lower holes. This gives you just nine notes. Yet a combination of these can produce marches to stir the most docile to rage bloody battle, reels to inspire the happiest of playful contented merriment, or laments to bring a tear to the eye of even the hardest of hearts. There are even lullabies, although to be practical these would have to be performed at some distance, it has to be said. But The Pipes are not a simple instrument. The skirly bits and diddly bits heard between the notes, known as grace notes, and seemingly just there to frustrate people like me trying to learn the bloody things, have their reasons. Maybe it's a way of filtering out those who are not true Believers, those who are not for The Cause. Whatever, your chanter is what you learn the instrument on, and learn new tunes with. It's basically a smaller holed, and much quieter, more environmentally friendly shall we say, practice version of the Pipe Chanter which is the business end of the bagpipes where your fingers lie. One cannot progress to the Main Instrument without first mastering the Practice Chanter, and obviously it is handy later in life for those spare moments, say, waiting at the bus stop in the morning, when you can whip it out of your briefcase to make sure your 'Highland Laddie' is as nice and tight as it should be. Your Chanter is for life. It is not a toy. Take as much care of it as you would your one-week old baby daughter, or the Crown Jewels.

In J & R Glen there were all manner of wooden tubes, piled up on various shelves, numbered and tagged, from the incredibly dusty floor to the ancient wood panelled roof. Some had holes in them, some not. There were lathes and wood turning tools through the back, and chippings and sawdust all over the room. The whole place had very much a lived-in look, like an eccentric inventor's garden shed. A sense of anticipation floated around, coupled with a strange musky scent, which made me feel that this truly was an important day in my life. Or was it impending doom?

I have the chanter my father bought for me that day on my desk as I write this, the ivory detail yellowed with age, and I remember Young Mr Glen taking time to show me around the shop, explaining how the African Blackwood that bagpipes are made of was turned on the lathe to the correct diameter, and then left to mature for forty years. Yes, that took me by surprise too - remember I'm only seven years old at this point - and bizarrely for a minute I thought I would have to wait forty years for the Real Deal. No such luck, as the numbers on the shelves were actually the years the wood was laid down, like a fine port. I really liked that shop, and old Young Mr Glen, and I would return only once before he retired. After chewing through the ivory tip of my bagpipe blowpipe aged about twelve - well, it was already worn anyway - the resultant Heimlich Manoeuvre by a guest at the Anstruther Rotary Club Christmas Dance probably saved my life. More importantly though, it gave me the great pleasure of watching old Young Mr Glen personally turn and carve a new blowpipe tip, right in front of me, out of a solid block of ivory.

Out of the shop then, and down the Royal Mile and there, of all things, is a busking Piper! Of course, this has suddenly become of immense interest to me, and I strain to understand how such a painful noise can possibly be called music. Maybe when I learn I can use earplugs, or play standing next to a road drill, or a Harrier jump jet. I clutch my new chanter, and watch this guy's fingers move in awe. Not possible, I say to my dad. No can do. But Dad is beaming and nodding at random passers-by, as if to say: "That will be my boy soon, you'll see!" Often when I'm 'tuning up' around the corner from Parliament Square Registry Office in anticipation of the arrival of some friend of a friend's wedding party, I will be tossed the odd two pence piece, and how insulting is that? I usually keep the money though.

Our final port of call was a small traditional Scottish jewellery shop that sold all manner of brooches, pendants and such like, and the odd tartan scarf or tie. We were attended to by a woman who looked like someone's auntie, in a floor length purple tartan skirt and a billowing white blouse who smelt of lavender. There were all manner of interesting objects in glass display cases, such as two handled *quaichs* for drinking out of, and some rather handy looking *sgian dubhs*, all twinkling brightly to attract the buyer. A long cane in the corner with a silver top inlaid with a large single cairngorm jewel looked particularly handsome. Maybe Dad could swap it for the dodgy old squint wooden thing he used to bring the cows in on the farm.

Despite my obvious suggestion, I was deemed to be too young for The Dagger just yet, but as if to mark the sense of occasion, I was given a Kilt Pin. This could be a tacky affair like the claw or paw off some animal, such as a badger, whose head was probably made into a sporran to adorn the nether regions of an officer in the Argyll and Sutherland Highlanders. Mine, however was a simple broad sword in sterling silver, just like William Wallace's, only smaller of course, which was very cool indeed. I suppose I could always use it as a weapon, if need be, but I would have to be careful to re- attach it through the same holes in the kilt, along the line of the tartan, on the lower right-hand side, as is the proper way.

Back in the car, heading over the Forth Road Bridge with all the windows open to get rid of the smell of the Orient mixed with stomach acid, I wonder what is next on the chanter front. Perhaps I could glue a piece of wood to the side and pretend it's a Sten gun, or simply poke someone in the eye with it. However, I strongly suspect I'm going to have to learn to play it. In the meantime then, apart from a small dry cleaning bill, it has been a successful day out. Clothes and 'stuff' for Mum, and, for Captain Jardine, well he was eagerly expecting a new Piper in the family, sometime soon.

Chapter 2. The Box

*"A box without hinges, key or lid
Yet golden treasure inside, is hid."*

Bilbo Baggins

Pipe Major Bert Barron, my new instructor (never teacher - it's a military thing), was an imposing man, but with a very friendly manner and an extremely shiny, bald head. Dad took to him at once as they were both ex-Black Watch, although Dad was post-war Territorial Army, and Pipey had a stack of medals having been a World War 2 veteran. And he had a British Empire Medal, for services to piping no less. He was the most approachable of men and would answer to the moniker of Pipey by me, as well as the more formal Pipe Major by Dad. Pipey would always refer to Dad as Captain Jardine, but then that is the way of rank and tradition. He was the most respected piper of his day, and his son Roderick won every competition in his path, so I had the best teacher 'in the land' as Pipey would say. Which meant Scotland. Which meant The World.

Of course, I was unaware of the emergence of pipe bands in other countries around the world back then; I mean, why, for God's sake would they possibly want to? The bands in the USA, proudly wearing their kilts back to front, were particularly keen in those days, and I'm glad to say they have improved somewhat, but nowhere near as good as the old Empire outposts of Canada, Kenya, Hong Kong and the Ghurkhas of Nepal. But if you think a well-trained Scottish lad straining away like constipation in a kilt on a street corner in Inverness sounds painful, you should get yourself over to Dunedin, Florida, USA (twinned with Stirling, Scotland, UK), for their annual Highland Games, and a truly memorable experience. This is the most hilarious thing you will ever hear. I'm laughing out loud, just remembering how truly awful this was. Basically, they taught themselves from 'teach yourself' books brought back from holiday in 'Scatland', and that is a serious, serious, mistake. Other, civilized, countries fly over an ex-Pipe Major or two and pay them serious money to do the job properly.

Even I have taught - sorry, instructed - in Taiwan of all places and I have the scars to prove it, but that's another story which I will cover later.

But it gets worse. A proper set of new (just turned forty years old) handmade bagpipes - and there is no other kind - will set you back around £750, and if you want the silver and all the trimmings, (minus the real ivory of course, that's now illegal), you can double that. By the same token, a Gibson Les Paul electric guitar will cost more than £1700, but you are not going to buy one of these babies to learn on. So the uninitiated buy the cheap novelty, almost toy pipes, that peddlers sell to gullible tourists on the Royal Mile during the Edinburgh Festival, along with Haggis snares for that trip Up North, a bottle of genuine 'air' from Roslyn Chapel, and a cuddly Loch Ness monster toy. That's along with a 'Teach Yourself the Great Highland Bagpipe In Ten Easy Steps' (fully illustrated, includes DVD), to go with the plastic octopus-like thing with the tartan pyjamas, that, when blown, sound like a small lamb with the beginnings of a throat infection, who has lost its mother on a rather wet and blustery day in Caithness.

But now, I had a chanter from the best Pipe Maker 'in the land', and I had the best Pipe Major in the land showing me how to use it. It was all getting rather exciting, and Pipey informed me that my First Tune... would be something called -'Scots Wha Hae'. If I was excited at this most momentous moment of a young Piper's life, Dad looked like he had just been knighted by the Queen, or that I had been knighted, or both. He positively beamed. Remember this was a man reliving his youth through me, and he had actually *wanted* to play the damn things, so you can picture the scene. Years later I would lead the Scottish Schools Pipe Bands out over the drawbridge of Edinburgh Castle, in front of the General Officer Commanding Scotland and I would see that same look of pride on Dad's face. It would only be then that I would forgive him for having to learn the bloody instrument in the first place.

Anyway, back to 'Scots Wha Hae'. Scots Who Have, in Old Scots. Odd name for one of piping's dreariest old asthmatic, wheezy tunes ever. It is actually a poem by the great Scottish poet Robert Burns, the first verse being:

"Scots wha hae wi' Wallace bled
Scotsman Bruce has often led
Scotland's off to war with England again
And to victorie, we hope."

Or something along those lines. I've never been a fan of Burns, but of course Burns' poetry is another of these fiercely Nationalistic passions of the Scots. To come out of the closet and admit that, in actual fact, he's a tad boring, is tantamount to admitting to actually quite enjoy the odd single malt whisky and Diet Coke in a tall glass, or expressing the opinion that Robert the Bruce was a coward. It simply isn't done. The only way I can sit through a Burns Supper these days, is to drink copious amounts of whisky before, during, and after the dreaded 'Address to The Haggis'. I need to be legless before 'The Reply from The Lassies' so I can fall asleep into my 'warm, reekin', rich', and 'reekin' being the operative word here, plate of haggis. I once told some sceptical Americans in a bar in Boston what was in it, and they agreed wholeheartedly that that was precisely why we only eat it once a year, on Burns Night. Having said that there is a hotel in Ayrshire, near Burns' birthplace, that hosts a

Supper every month. Popular and revered though he is, they are most welcome to it.

However, playing a Burns song is better than listening to some old codger read it out to a captive audience, with the possible exception of 'Scots Wha Hae'. Half pished Hogmanay revellers will often shout out a request for it because the name sounds so, well, Scottish, as in: "Allan, gie's a bit o' Scots Whey Hey! Whey, Hey! You're the Man! Wha's like us Scots!" Then when you play it, everyone gets misty-eyed and sways from side to side, nodding knowingly into the distance, remembering the purple of the heather they once saw, on a painting in their grannie's spare room.

The reason that this particular tune is most often used as a First Tune, is that it is a simple Slow March, containing all the most basic 'finger work' necessary for the novice piper to get up and running. Or more accurately 'chanterer' as you are nowhere near The Pipes yet, my friend. This soon becomes alarmingly apparent after an attempt at the first two bars.

Now to get your head around the frustration of learning this instrument, think of this. Your first attempt at the first two bars of this tune will come after your first two months of tuition. Yes, two months of doing what, exactly, you say, Well you are learning all the Other Stuff which makes pipe music sound the way it does: the grace note groupings, the Doublings, the Triplets, the Grip, the Throw on the D for instance, and not forgetting, amongst other things, the discussion at length of the importance of the Birl. Especially since there is usually always a Birl at the end of every tune ever written. Listen out for it if you will. Yes, all these and more, such as the incredibly complicated taorluath and crunluath, in amongst the pentatonic scale have to be dealt with and perfected at this early stage, and just when you think you've cracked it, Pipey decides that it is Time, and the Scots Guards Standard Settings of Pipe Music is turned to the appropriate page for good old 'Scots Who Have'. Can you play it? Can you hell.

Think of it like this. You are now at a stage in your piping career where you have learnt to stand up, walk a few steps, and fall down without hurting yourself. Next you will be up for a three-wheeler bike for some light running around the back garden, followed by a two-wheeler, with stabilisers. Then, stabilisers off, a small mountain bike with a huge crash helmet and knee pads for that Sunday trip to the park with the family. Eventually your first skateboard, then a Provisional Driving Licence by God, and finally you are let loose on the open roads. Then Pipey will decide that it's time to enter a competition, and then you will have finally moved up into the realms of Formula One Racing.

One day, Dad came home clutching a mysterious wooden box under his arm. As we crowded round to see what might be in it, he gestured us to back off, as the bodyguard of a rock star would to some over-enthusiastic fans. The leather handle on the box was broken, which is why he had been carrying it under his arm, and the lid was held in place by two metal fasteners, and both they and the one remaining hinge were very rusty. With great anticipation, we gave the man his space. Then, and very slowly, he opened The Box.

Inside was a pile of dusty old wooden tubes, of varying shapes and sizes, with a strange aura surrounding them, and certainly a strange odour emanating from them. Some were the same size as others, usually in groups of three. One in particular had a line of holes along it. Suddenly, a flash back to J & R Glen's shop told me what this was. This, was a 'set' of Pipes!

Not in the conventional sense, however. There was no bag for a start; it had long since rotted away, or more likely been eaten by rats, which I could see was going to be a fundamental problem. Also, the tubes looked far less pristine than the ones in the shop, and the shop ones were up to forty years old. It turned out that Dad had paid 'a man in the pub' £50 for that box of tubes, and he was now in that state he would get in on Christmas Day, when he would push me out of the way so that he could build a crane out of my new Meccano set.

We've all seen this with dads, but mine was a particular 'boy with a toy' kind of guy. I wouldn't have minded, but later I could never figure out how to build a crane as good as his, which was so frustrating. So Dad, being Dad aged twelve, at once set about trying to figure out which tube went where. The rest of us looked on bemused, as with trademark tongue sticking out slightly, and on hands and knees, he got to work. After some time, and through much trial and error, a semblance began to emerge, which bore absolutely no resemblance to the Highland Bagpipe whatsoever. The frown on Dad's face now was more to do with the fact that he was beginning to think he might have been conned by the man in the pub, and let's face it, the assorted brown tubes on the floor looked like they had come from a toilet roll factory, rather than the makers of a prestigious military instrument.

Specialist help was therefore required, and the next day Dad drove me, and the box of dodgy old bagpipe tube things, to the Pipe Major's house in St. Andrews, where he was the caretaker for the local University Officer Training Corps. I liked this old building, which was a drill hall for the cadets, as well as housing Pipey and his family, and Bracken, the big, woolly golden retriever who was always pleased to greet any visitors. When I started going there at weekends for extracurricular lessons, on top of the ones he was teaching me at school, I would look forward to the last ten minutes or so, before Dad came to pick me up. That's when the struggle with the complexity of the first two bars of 'Scots Wha Hae', the easiest of pipe tunes in the book, and the monotony of the repetition of scales and various movements to improve dexterity, and therefore, 'finger work', would end.

Pipey would, in a hushed and quavering voice and with expansive arm gestures, tell me stories of the Great Battles, and of the Great Pipers 'in the land'. Like two kids playing at smugglers, we would often tip-toe down some secret passage, and open a secret cupboard, wherein I would be shown, amid great excitement and ceremony, the most magnificent of bejewelled rams head snuff box. The horns were inlaid with silver, carved in the styles, I was told, of Celtic, runic, and the thistle. Or, with much reverence and solemnity, open the glass case containing the Russian standard captured by C company, 8th Cameronians, at Balaclava. Pipey's big old house was full of such treasures. I was sure he must have siphoned them off from many a Regimental Sergeants' Mess over a period of many years. It is well known that all the best swag of this sort can be found on display in the Sergeants' Mess as opposed to the Officers' Mess, as well as the better quality and variation of victuals and whiskies. This is due to the fact that the President of an Officers' Mess is usually a young Subaltern, having the duty thrust upon him by his peers and elders, whereas the wily Sergeants have many years' experience in the dubious and mysterious art of 'procurement' as they might refer to it.

And so the great Pipe Major cast his expert, beady eye over the contents of The Box, and proudly declared them to be Hendersons. I looked blankly at him, the significance of this being totally lost on me. Dad had that look of a schoolboy who has put up his hand in class, although not knowing the answer to the teacher's question. A 'fine maker of The Pipes' apparently, if not one of the best 'in the land'. Well, that's a turn up, I was thinking. Hendersons, no less. Captain Jardine was being assured that Pipey would personally take care of the restoration project, one that I would be involved in as part of my training, sort of like learning to field strip a weapon before firing it. I was curious to know how they worked, and why they were so loud and awful sounding, and I thought it would be fun to field strip them, say, at Christmas, and watch Dad struggle woefully to put them back together again.

A week or so later and we were off to St. Andrews again, to pick up my new pipes. A new box had been bought for them, wooden with black leather covering, metal corners and locking catches, and with absolutely no expense spared, my initials painted on the lid by the local painter and decorator, who also liked to be thought of as a signwriter. ATJ for Allan Thomas Jardine. Dad's initials were TAJ for Thomas Allan Jardine, but he was known as Allan so as not to be confused with my grandfather, Thomas Jardine Jr. Some of the older villagers back in Fife call me 'Wee Allan' as opposed to Big Allan to this day.

Moving on, there are such things as 'half sets', designed for very young players (or maybe very small players), but don't go near them. When you grow up a bit you will only have to move on to a 'full set' anyway and have to figure out how to stop the things sliding off your shoulder all over again. These pipes were a 'full set' and what a magnificent set they were, after some TLC from Pipey. There was smooth, creamy ivory and gleaming silver, over the shining brown wood, which was Cocus wood, and a very rare wood to be used for bagpipes, imported from the West Indies. A new goatskin bag had been tied to the 'stocks'. Sheepskin might be preferred as this is a more supple skin, but the heavier goat hide is more durable. These days modern technology means that bags can be made of Goretex or other materials from the realms of science fiction, reducing the need for maintenance and the ever-present threat of bronchitis, botulism or worse from spores festering within the infamous air supply unit which gives the instrument its name. The stocks are the parts which in turn hold the bass and two tenor drones that lie across the shoulder, the blowpipe, and the all-important Pipe Chanter that hangs underneath. The bag was clothed, appropriately, in a Black Watch tartan cover. The drones were separated and held apart by a fine rope of white silk chord. All in all, I'd say they were worth far more than the fifty quid Dad had paid for them, and to this day I've never had them valued, in case the shock might be too much. To think I once inadvertently left them in a stripper bar in Fort Lauderdale as well.

All of a sudden, and much to my surprise, and indeed alarm, Pipey sneakily had them plastered all over me in an instant. The ivory tipped blowpipe was thrust into my mouth, and instructions to "Put your left hand like that, on the chanter" and "Not like that, laddie, bring yer shoulder round, that's the way!" and "Stand up straight, man! Ye cannae be a Piper all hunched up like ye've got the lumbago!" But that was enough for one day, and the technique of the delivery of the air from the lungs to the stuff that makes all the racket was for the next lesson.

On the way home I reflected on my increasingly bizarre collection of equipment on the musical (hopefully) front. I had a chanter, the pipes, the Scots Guards Standard Settings of Pipe Music, binding thread, spare reeds, rubber stoppers, a lump of sealing wax and a bottle of gunky stuff called Bag Seasoning. This was Pipey's own secret recipe and smelt like embalming fluid and quite probably was, as its job was to keep the bag supple and air tight. To cap it all I also had my own personalised box to keep it all in. If I could just get the first two bars of 'Scots Wha Hae' to sound anything unlike a funeral march played at half speed, and more like it was supposed to, I was laughing.

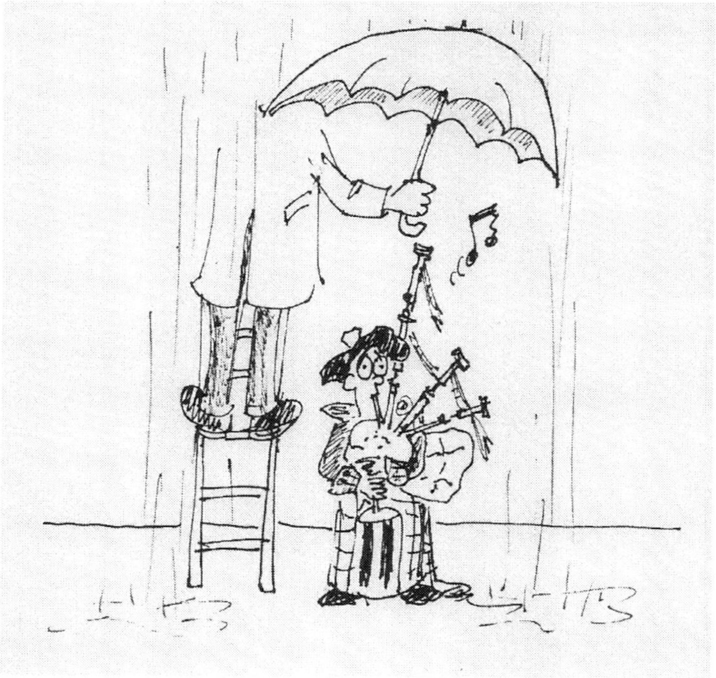

Chapter 3. The Two Tables

"Ah, Haggis. Chopped heart and lungs cooked in a wee sheep's stomach. Tastes as good as it sounds!"
Wullie the Scots Janitor in *The Simpsons*

Talking of laughing, I always have a giggle when I pass my pipes over to someone big and strong, and watch their face slowly turn puce, and veins erupt in their neck as they try to get more than a tired moan out of them. Especially if you are nine years old and that person is your dad. Once I had tamed The Beast and could rattle off 'Scots Wha Hae' as well as 'The Green Hills of Tyrol', 'The Skye Boat Song' and, aptly perhaps, 'The Battle's O'er' you just knew he couldn't resist having a go himself.

My father, like most people's fathers I suppose, was a man who knew the answer to everything a young boy could ever ask, such as how people could speak down a telephone cable, or how a pane of glass was made from sand, or, and I could never figure this out, how he knew there was a litter of tiny new born kittens, hidden an extremely inaccessible part of the old and redundant threshing machine on the farm. I mean what on earth was he doing in there in the first place to discover that? I once watched him take a tractor apart and put it back together again in an afternoon. Indeed, with our new combine harvester, never were we happiest, when an entire summer's day was spent dismantling the whole front end in a field, because Dad's pipe had fallen out of his mouth and got caught in the workings.

But get even a squeak out of the bagpipes he could not, so let me explain. It's like pushing a car, in that if you shoulder barge it, it is not going to budge, and you'll have a sore shoulder. But, once steady pressure is applied, it will move, and one man can push a one-ton car along a road. So with The Pipes it is the same technique. Once full of air, with a decent bit of initial puff admittedly, a sharp tap to the bag kicks in the reeds, and then you simply breathe with a firm steady pressure. Then you don't squeeze it all out again, the mere weight of your left arm on the bag gives enough pressure, coupled with the tension from the expanded skin, to allow the player to take a swift intake of air. A small valve in the blowpipe stops air rushing out when you take a breath, as you start the process again, indefinitely. Especially in the case of playing *Piobaireachd*, pronounced 'peebroch', which to young ears seem to last for months, or even years. This 'music' really is a world-beating cure for insomnia, and I will tell you more about it, but suffice to say that this method of bag and blowing steadily can mean that a piper can play on and on, and on, and on. And on, and on. Visit Edinburgh during the Festival to see if I'm lying, or read the story of poor Bill Millen, who was Lord Lovat's personal piper at the D-Day landings. The defending Germans felt so sorry for him playing away continually amongst the bullets, up to his neck in water, that they cut him a break and didn't shoot at him.

So now I was officially a Piper, and because of all the extra lessons and practice of roughly an hour a day in the back garden, not to mention the frequent: "Right Allan, give us a wee tune then" scenarios when my parents' friends would pop round, I was actually becoming quite good. Pipey even grandly gave me a medal, from a shoe box full of them which he kept in the dresser in his dining room. Surely more swag, I suspected, but it was hallmarked silver, and I was very proud of it. It was promptly taken off me to be sent to the engravers, who fashioned a bar for it with my name on, and inscribed with the legend 'Piping'. I still wear it to this day, on my black dress kilt jacket.

Around this time, aged ten by now, it was decided that I had become so proficient that I would perform at my first Burns Supper. Now I don't know who was behind this plot, or who was getting a fee for this, but it certainly wasn't me. And I had to learn a new tune, another Burns effort called 'A Man's A Man For A' That!' I was beginning to resent my parents' opportunistic use of me, as a sort of organ grinders monkey, in tartan, but what could I do but go along. After all I had never before performed in front of such an audience, at The Golf Hotel in Elie, no less, and the adrenaline was starting to flow.

The upside was that I was given a new sporran, the old one being the size of a pack of playing cards from when I was four, and a new pair of Brogue shoes, which were the best ever. They had leather soles, and were festooned, for want of a better word, with what we called in those days 'segs'. Small metal tackets that made sparks if you scuffed them along the pavement. They were designed to preserve the life of the expensive leather sole, especially if one was in the habit of scuffing one's soles along the pavement.

I could sense my parents' anxiousness that all should be well on the night, because as well as the new gear, my folded-up kilt hem was lowered by the tailors, to adjust to my growth. I was always told that the bottom of your kilt should rest half way across the kneecap, or when kneeling it should just touch the floor. My hem had started off being folded up inside half as long as the kilt itself, but if I grew a few more inches it would have to be a whole new kilt as well, and hopefully one in a better looking tartan than the hideous brown and black that were the Jardine colours at that time. Maybe, to afford all this Pipe nonsense, they were getting a return by selling me into the slavery of the Burns cause. Anyhow, I soon found myself, one evening around late January, in a very steamy hotel kitchen indeed.

Kitchens are busy and stressful places to be at the best of times, and I really felt like I was getting in the way. I could have offered to stir one of the vast steel pots of mashed turnip, or 'neeps', but my most immediate concern was watching *Top of the Pops* on a small portable television by the sink. I should have been stressed by the steamy atmosphere affecting my pipes sensitive tuning, or that it was making my hair go curly, or that the stench of the haggis was taking the shine off my new shoes, but I was more concerned with who would be top of the popular music charts. You see it was getting near Show Time for the Burns Supper nonsense, but I really wanted to see what was what on the telly. Then, just as that week's heroes were announced as being Number One, it was Game On for the entrance of The Haggis, or 'Piping in the Haggis' as it is properly known. The Head Chef carrying this enormous ugly thing, like a giant, sweaty slug, with a paper Saltire flag sticking out of it, was saying: "Ready when you are, son!" It was time to fill the bag with puff, strike up, and off out through the swing doors, and beyond.

This was at once very different, and most surreal. Once out of the heat of the kitchen, and after a last agonizing glance at Mud playing *Tiger Feet* on the telly, two vast lines of grinning, be-tartan clad grown up folk were staring at me, and starting to clap. I did not know whether to play in time to the clapping, or stand my ground and play 'A Man's A Man' at the speed it was supposed to be played, so I kind of compromised in the middle somewhere, and marched confidently once around the two long tables running the length of the room, before lining up to go between them to the 'Top Table'. This is where I would stop and the haggis would be presented to the President for the Address, a Burns ramble in old Scots words to describe the beauty and majesty of this thing that was about to be ceremoniously divided up and eaten. I was belting out my all, strutting my stuff in the new gear, the adults gazing down on me sweetly like I was a Crufts puppy. I knew my parents were in there somewhere, but I couldn't see, as your head is kind of held in place by the blowpipe stuck in your mouth, so you can only use peripheral vision. For this very reason, never, and I repeat never, play pipes when walking down a staircase. The one and only time

I ever did this was at a 21st birthday bash in The Tayside Hotel in Dundee, and I fell and fractured a bone in my foot. Second last stair it was as well.

I could not see him, but I could sense the chef behind me, no doubt carrying his 'Great Chieftain O' The Puddin' Race' aloft to the baying crowd, who by now are near hysterical with anticipation, and egged on by a good slosh of whisky. Clap, clap. Stamp, stamp. Ear shattering noise from a swaggering wee boy. And then... the swagger stopped. And the noise. And the clapping. For my pristine, seg endowed, tackety shoes had left the carpeted area of the Function Suite, and had hit the exposed, polished wood of the dance floor, up till now hidden under the tables and which I had not anticipated. I went arse over tit in spectacular fashion, backwards, taking down the Head Chef on the way, who was by now on his back with the silver salver upturned. It looked like the Haggis must have exploded upon impact with the floor, and was absolutely everywhere. I'll never forget the mixture of horror and disbelief on Chef's face as he tried to disentangle himself from a small boy with haggis in his hair, who in turn was entangled in a very nice set of bagpipes, with a Black Watch cover. Oops.

I was surprised that I was not in the doghouse after such an inauspicious start to my public performance career. I felt terrible that I may have totally humiliated my parents in front of their friends, however Dad later confessed to finding the whole affair vastly amusing. I thought that maybe they wouldn't make me play in front of people again, but in fact it was quite the opposite. As word of my prowess spread, it seemed to me I was the only piper in Fife, apart from Pipey and his son Roderick of course. Dad took me to see these guys perform at a wedding once. They wore matching Full Dress Ceremonial outfits, the only difference being Pipey's war medals, and of course his four upside down chevrons on the sleeve, to denote the rank of Pipe Major. I bet they charged a fortune, and they certainly looked the part, but for me, it was turning out to be freebies all the way. Unless maybe my parents were stashing the loot in a trust fund for me, which I doubted.

No, this was time to claw back the investment, in the form of the prestige and importance that a family was accorded, on account of having a piper available, for free hire, to everyone's weddings, funerals, school sports days, Women's Institute meetings, political rallies, boat launches, barbecues, or farmers' markets. Silence was but a distant memory at garden fetes, harbour festivals, christenings, Great Uncle Neil's birthday party, VE Day celebrations or Children's Gala processions the length and breadth of the East Nuke of Fife. If I could have been driven as far as New York for the 4th of July, you would have heard me wailing mercilessly away on Fifth Avenue, whilst trying to dodge the traffic.

Of course, as I continued to learn new tunes, I had a less boring repetoire, both for me and for everyone else, and especially our next-door neighbours, the poor sods. The problem was I had absolutely no control over what I could play. People would insist on me playing the *White Heather Club* stuff they liked such as 'My Home' or 'The Rowan Tree', as opposed to the more faster, aggressive, warmongering "Charge ye bastards!" tunes that I favoured, and that the pipes were designed for, such as 'Scotland the Brave' or 'The Cock of the North' or 'Come and Have a Go If You Think Yer Hard Enough'.

There has been much debate recently as to a new, or rather more accurately a definitive, Scottish National Anthem, and I think we should revert to 'Scotland the Brave' and stop this 'Flower of Scotland' church hymn nonsense. The Scottish comedian Billy Connolly famously suggested the theme tune from *The Archers* radio programme as a substitute for 'God Save the Queen' as the English and British anthem and what's so funny about that? At least it fits into the nine-note scale of the Highland Bagpipe, unlike 'Flower of Scotland'. I know this, and don't tell anyone, because I secretly tried out 'Archers' for a laugh even though it's not a proper pipe tune at the Stockbridge Duck Race once in amongst other stuff, and no one noticed!

Sorry, I digress again. One day it was decided that I should be entered into my first competition, the Scottish Junior Championships, conveniently held in St. Andrews. The noise of hundreds of boys - very few girls played then - busily tuning the bass and two tenor drones to be in perfect harmony with the 'Low A' note of the chanter, and practising completely different Marches, Strathspeys and Reels all at the same time, was one that caught me surprise. Think of the noise of a large penguin colony in Antarctica, only louder, more discordant, and with a slightly higher pitch. And, in amongst all this cacophony, like the penguin mother listening out for the cries of its chick, Pipey tracked me down to offer some valuable last-minute advice, like making sure my laces were securely tied, as we did not want another 'slip up', and to not pick my nose while waiting in the wings to go on.

You would think that having been practising the same three damn tunes over and over again in the back garden, rain, hail or shine would have given me confidence, but by now I was simply petrified. Not for the first time came that wave of utter resentment towards my parents for all this totally unnecessary suffering, not to mention a complete waste of my time. If it was today, I would be straight on the phone to Childline to report them for child abuse.

I remember in each of the classes of 'Under 15', 'Under 18' and 'Under 21' was one of three brothers from Prestonpans, known in piping circles simply as 'The Brothers'. They were so very good, and always won everything so why should anyone else want to bother? Roderick Barron, of course, always won the 'Past Winners'. Anyway, before I knew it my name was being called, and it was Game On once again. I nervously entered Stage Left with a very odd feeling in the pit of my stomach. This was it. Months of practising the same three tunes over and over again, under the patient coaching of my learned Instructor, had led me to this point. I reckoned this is what it must feel like for a sprinter on the starting blocks at the Olympic Games. All that work, and in ten seconds' time maybe glory, or maybe not.

I was immediately surprised at how high up I was on the stage as I gazed over the audience, the air pregnant with expectation, and that everything had suddenly gone very, very quiet. I felt so alone. The only sound was of one of the three old and austere judges, tapping his pencil on his teeth, thoughtfully. If these bastards were trying to put me off with their piercing gaze going through me like a shard of ice, it was nearly working.

And so then, for what seemed like the millionth time in my life I struck up once more, and strode into 'Captain Norman Orr Ewing', a typical four-part, kilt swinging, military March, and in my opinion a March should be, well, marched. My Strathspey that day was 'Loudon's Bonnie Woods and Braes' and I'm fairly certain my Reel was 'The High Road to Linton'. These were rousing little numbers compared to the others playing the more complicated, dreary eight-part monstrosities that are slightly slower, possibly to fit in the vast amount of ridiculously complicated finger work. These tunes exist simply to allow people like the 'The Brothers' of this world, and quite probably the parents of those concerned, to show off in competitions. You wouldn't want them played at your wedding, that's for sure. Like a dog riding a skateboard, it is all very impressive but what's the point? Pursuit of perfection and honouring the great masters of the Art, obviously, but remember I'm still just a wee laddie.

Suddenly it was all over, and polite applause rippled through the audience as I climbed down the stage steps, relieved and sweating, to join my parents for the rest of the show. Dad enthusiastically pointed out that when I was giving my rendition of 'Captain Norman Orr Ewing', the judges stopped scribbling furiously, put their feet up, their hands behind their heads, and simply listened. They were chilling out as a young boy played a simple song that was a huge chasm away from the terribly serious stuff of the other kids who had, I discovered, been learning from their Pipe Major dads since as early as the age of four, and practiced two hours a day. Every day. I thought I had it tough, poor bastards.

More importantly I did however, and this was indeed a shock to us all, win the prize for 'Marching and Deportment'. My swagger to a simple tune had shown them all up! Before I knew it, I was making my way to the stage, applause ringing in my ears, to collect a new practice chanter with an engraved shield on it. Not the best start in the world of Formula 1, but a Podium Finish nonetheless. And now I had two practice chanters! The Brothers only had poxy cups, which they had to hand back for the next years' winners. Themselves, naturally. But then I was not at all worried, as next year I would go on to win the "Marching and Deportment' again, naturally.

NY ♥ THE BLACK WATCH
I appreciate this is Tartan week
Pipe McPhail, but Colonel Bogey is not a pipe tune!

Chapter 4. The Hogmanay Incident

"Traditions are just things that people with no imagination look forward to."

Diane Morgan

Thirty-first December. Hogmanay. The most quintessential of Scottish celebrations, and an excuse for an almighty piss up, usually in the home, or better, someone else's home. This is so that you can throw up in their garden, and not your own. Hogmanay is, and always will be, the Big One. No other nation on earth celebrates the New Year like the Scots, and no nation gets as drunk, which means embracing all the patriotism that goes with it. It is no surprise that Scotland has, as public holidays, the 1st and 2nd of January off work as opposed to England's 1st only. We need the extra day to recover. Of course, it has changed a bit these days, in that no one on Princes Street in Edinburgh at midnight, at 'The Bells' is actually from Edinburgh, or indeed Scotland, but seemingly from every other country, terrestrial or otherwise. In the villages people now at least close, if not lock, their doors before venturing out to 'first foot' the neighbours.

It's all a bit embarrassing really. Men will don ill-fitting £20 kilts for the occasion, in a soccer team tartan, or dig out the particularly cheap and nasty one they wore to the last Scotland rugby game. Let's face it, you wouldn't wear your good one. The girls just get all tarted up, the order of the day being to snog an unsuspecting policeman. I apologise that my own kilt gear kit is, I have to admit, a bit threadbare of late.

All my jacket buttons are different, and if you look closely, the middle tassel of my dress sporran is a shade darker than the other two as I lost the original falling out of a taxi. This is because when the Scots celebrate, a lot of alcohol is involved, the kilt is involved, and the Pipes are invariably involved. It stands to reason, therefore, that I am involved.

So here we are then, 31st December 1974, about one in the morning, and our house is full of noisy, drunken revelry. We lived in a big house in the next-door village of Lower Largo by this time, having inherited it from my late Great Uncle Jim, and it was always the focus of attention of all things Hogmanay. It also had its very own, and very sleepy, thirteen-year-old piper at the door to serenade the guests as they arrived in their varying states of intoxication, clutching booze and Black Bun. Ah, yes, Black Bun. I'll never know what my grandmother put in hers, but I do remember it tasted absolutely awful. If you can imagine a block of solidified diesel oil with some manky old raisins in it you are coming close to the experience. It is another mysterious and highly suspect foodstuff that is only eaten once a year, like haggis. Maybe we should eat the Bun on Burns night with the Haggis, and get the gagging over with in one go.

It was interesting to watch your friends' parents, normally respectable adults, carrying on like chimps at a graduation ball. A heavy thud to the left of me signalled the slipping of Mr R on a mat in the dining room doorway. He rose quickly before he thought anyone had noticed, and was now looking around in vain for the fat cigar he was sure he had been smoking, not realising, as I could see from my vantage point, that it was stuck to his arse. Suddenly I was instructed to 'Go and find your dad!' I was reluctant to leave my post, as I wanted to witness the reaction of Mr R when that flattened, but still smouldering cigar burned through to bare skin, but I propped my pipes up on a chair and went for a wander.

There were a lot of rooms in that house, mostly full of people I barely recognised. They all seemed to know me for some reason, so it was a case of lots of firm hand shaking from the men, and big hugs and slobbery kisses from women, who reeked of a pungent mix of perfume and Campari. I would have sneaked off to my bed but there was too much noise. Eventually I ended up in the kitchen, where there were two little old ladies who had evidently taken it upon themselves to wash glasses, and carry out plates of the dreaded Black Bun to the masses. That's when I spotted Dad.

Now my father 'liked a dram' as much as the next man, and as I explained earlier Hogmanay is a time in the calendar where we, in Scotland, 'like a dram'. Or two even, or maybe seven or eight? Whatever, when one is entertaining in one's house, there is a line of drunkenness that should not be crossed. Dad had evidently galloped across that line in spectacular style and was now passed out on the floor by the kitchen sink, with his kilt over his head, revealing The Secret of what is worn beneath. Remember the two little old ladies? They had merrily, and I suppose they were a bit tiddly, been stepping over him to get to the sink, and ignoring the fact that Dad was indeed a Black Watch soldier and very much a True Scotsman.

I was horrified at this most unfortunate of incidents, and threw a tartan rug over him as camouflage until I could decide what to do. But the word was out that the host was down, and with the music off and the air hanging heavy with smoke and gloom, the guests made their way elsewhere. I made my way to bed, the pipes back in their box. Poor Dad. His only crime was to be carried away on that great tide of emotion that is a Scottish Hogmanay, and we have all been there. We never had as big a New Year party again, which meant no more piping at the door till all hours. I will, however, always be sad that I had not been around to witness Mr R's reaction to that smouldering cigar.

Long after the 'incident' was forgotten, I had become aware, in September, of more sinister plotting behind my back. This time it was of a most evil nature, involving me being deported to something called a Public School, so called because any member of the public, who has the cash or is eligible for a bursary, can send their kid there, albeit for the promise of a fine education, and provided the child can pass the entrance exams. The institution in question was called Fettes College, which was also nicknamed 'The Eton of the North' due to the high reputation it enjoyed in Scotland, comparable to that grand institution south of the border. I was abandoned at the gates of this fabulous, Disneyland-styled building in Edinburgh, with a huge trunk of clothes and sporting equipment, which I could hardly lift, and my pipes of course, and a check list of certain places I had to be at a certain time. Since I had no idea where on earth in this massive campus these places were made the whole thing academic, but a chirpy, bespectacled, and very blond Belgian kid seemed to know his way around. He was most impressed with my leather soled brogues, and cheerfully showed me to my dormitory in School House in the main building, where he thankfully gave me a hand to hoist my trunk up a spiral staircase, and onto a bed. I chose one tucked away in a corner, in a turret, and that was to be home for me for the coming year.

After a few weeks I had sort of settled in, if you can call it that in a place like this, with its unwritten rules and traditions, and got to know some fellow pupils with broad Scottish accents who could actually understand what I was saying. So, one day I went off in search of The Pipe Band to offer my services, such as they were. The culture shock of attending a school such as this was that every day was a new adventure, but in an exciting way, and today would be no exception. The Band used an old classroom tucked away down a corridor, and at least I was in the right place for once, as the all too familiar reedy, nasal whine of a dozen practice chanters wafted from the room as I approached.

Inside there were all these adults, sitting around with their feet up on desks bearing a century's worth of carved initials and teachers caricatures. Some were playing, and some were idly chatting, expertly twirling their chanters through their fingers. I made a mental note to learn how to do this, and strode bravely into the room. 'Sir' I announced to a tall man with impressive sideburns, 'I have come to join The Band!' The tall guy was in fact only sixteen, and laughed when he assured me I did not have to call him 'Sir'. He was extremely gracious however, and informed me that the Band instructor, Mr Percival, would be arriving presently, and that some sort of audition might be on the agenda.

I was nervous instantly, but confident nonetheless. My theory was that as a winner of Marching and Deportment I could hold my own marching in a band, and people would not hear my bad playing in amongst all these other guys. I was secretly praying that they played 'Captain Norman Orr Ewing' which would be to my advantage.

All of a sudden it was feet off the table and chairs pulled up as, in the ensuing silence, the enigmatic John 'Jock' Percival, late of Edinburgh City Police Pipe Band walked slowly in. He had that presence, as all policeman do, of making you feel that you had done something wrong. I remember his shoes were very highly polished, and had steel heel caps that clicked menacingly as he walked, slowly, up to the desks. 'Gentleman' he whispered, a voice oozing authority and discipline, 'At ease'. He was walking around me now, sizing me up. He had well-oiled hair and an immaculately manicured moustache "And you are?"

"Jardine, sir. I have come to join The Band."

Silence in the room for a moment, then: "Have you indeed, Mr Jardine. Come on then laddie, let's see what you can do. Impress me. I'm all ears." Jock Percival took a seat at a desk, slicked back his hair, put his feet up, and was indeed all ears.

The corners of his mouth turned up in a slight smile as I marched up and down between the desks doing my set piece, coming to a well-executed halt in front of him for my Strathspey and Reel. "Very good laddie, you've been well taught. Who's your instructor?" On the information of the hallowed name of Pipe Major Bert Barron, BEM, he nodded sagely. A good piper, he mused, if not one of the best 'in the land'. And I was Pipey's protégé.

The next day at lunchtime I was eagerly off to the 'Corps Stores' to draw my first Full Dress Ceremonial uniform. The gentleman in charge here, I was told in hushed tones, was known as the Sergeant Major, as well as some other ruder nicknames. I got to know him well in later years, especially with the Shooting Team, but at this time I didn't know that his bark was worse than his bite. As an ex-Argyll and Sutherland Highlander quartermaster sergeant major, he fell into the school of: 'If I was meant to issue kit I would be called an Issuer, not a Storeman'. By the time I finished school at the age of eighteen, I would have the greatest respect for this old soldier, but at thirteen, I was petrified of him.

'Flashes, two; hose tops, two; spats, two; Glengarry, one; cross belt, one; plaid, one; brooch, one, securing the plaid, for the use of...' He barked over the counter, as he glared down at me, and I could not help but be curious as to why he wore his tie over the top of his jersey. Secretly I was very excited about all this new gear, and couldn't wait to hump it all back to my dorm to try it on. It all weighed so much I had to get a friend to give me a hand. First on was the most handsome dark blue tunic with silver buttons, or 'doublet', and at once we could see a very severe problem indeed. The sleeves covered my hands, so how would I be able to play? My pal tried in vain to roll them up at the cuff, but the cloth was too thick. Holding the Hunting Stewart kilt against me confirmed our worst suspicions that that, also, was way too big. We just assumed the plaid would be dragging along the ground behind me, like a bridal train. The sleeves on my school blazer were also over my hands, but, as I had to keep on explaining to some of the more wealthy kids, that was for me 'to grow into', and anyway I could always remove it to write while in class.

A dilemma indeed. No way was I going back to The Sergeant Major to complain his store did not adequately cater for a wee thirteen-year-old boy, who had made it into the big boys' band. My friend unhelpfully suggested using scissors, or a knife perhaps, to trim everything down, even the sporran, but how silly would that look? No, initiative and common sense prevailed. I remembered there was a pay phone on the wall in a corridor outside our house Reading Room. There was always a queue, and this evening, after Prep, there were the same sorry suspects. I asked them why they had to phone home so often, as they would see their parents in person in another thirteen weeks anyway. For me though this phone call was an emergency. It was time to Dial a Dad.

Neither Dad nor me were entirely sure if parental visits were actually allowed at this school; remember I had only been here a few weeks, but we both agreed that this was a situation that desperately needed rectifying. I did not want to arouse suspicion by asking permission from a teacher, so it was agreed that late on Sunday, after dark, Dad would go into stealth mode, and drive our car up to the old West Gate. This was generally locked to traffic, but I could secretly meet him just outside by climbing over with the offending articles hidden in a laundry bag. I had said the length of the kilt would not impede my playing, but no son of Dad's would be playing in a Pipe Band with his kilt hanging past his knees. I had an amusing vision of him with his face blacked out with camouflage cream, and wearing a black polo neck sweater and matching beret, so when I met him with the kit, I was relieved to see no camo cream, as I wouldn't have put it passed him. Then after a brief handshake the stuff was in the back seat of the car, and he was off into the night, like a ghost.

It was the same drill two days later, with not a word spoken as I accepted the large brown paper parcel, and waved him off into the darkness, hoping that he had not got my dimensions wrong, and got the tailor to take it in/up too short. But oh joy, it could all have been custom made for me, the only giveaway after I tried it all on, being the length of the long white horse hair sporran with its black tassles.

I have a photograph of me wearing that first band uniform, and I remember how proud I was to wear it, the Real Deal indeed. Years later, when I was by then wearing the coveted Pipe Major's uniform at that school, a shy wee thirteen-year-old boy, from Strachur if I remember rightly, joined the band. I asked how he had got on with the Sergeant Major when drawing his kit and he said everything had been fine, and that his uniform fitted perfectly. I laughed out loud, because it would, wouldn't it?

Camp Piper protection

Chapter 5. Air pistols at dawn.

"Practice as if you're the worst. Perform as if you're the best."

Mahatma Ghandi

Now, as a fully paid up member of the Fettes College Combined Cadet Force Pipes and Drums, with the lowly rank of Cadet, there was some serious shit going down as far as the tunes I had to learn. It was time for the eight-part monstrosities I mentioned earlier: the Competition Stuff, the Really Hard Stuff. Rubbing his hands, and with sadistic glee, Mr Percival announced the names of our March, Strathspey, and Reel for this summer's Scottish Schools competition. The names, 'Men of Argyll', 'Ca' The Ewes' and 'Thomsons Dirk' meant nothing to me, but the others in the room groaned, and looked crestfallen. Two years before, the competition was won by George Heriot's School with 'Thomsons Dirk' as their Reel, and everyone appreciated how tricky it was, and how brave Heriots were to gamble with it.

For once though, strangely, I did not mind any of this. You see, I was in a Band. A Band of Brothers, so to speak. We were all in this together, stuck in the same boat of the bagpipe. It was no longer just me against the world. Admittedly I was younger than everyone else, and the Pipe Major was even a School Prefect, one up from a House Prefect, so that was very scary. But somehow, in The Band, rank and age seniority ceased to matter; odd in a school where generally that sort of thing mattered a great deal. In fact, I am sure my peers in the dorm must have been impressed, what with the new uniform and being able to pass the time of day in a corridor with a School Prefect, although they never let on. So from now on every Tuesday and Thursday evenings were spent sitting with our chanters at the desks in that musty old classroom, roughly in a circle, with Mr Percival at the epicentre of all the whiney noise. My new friends were much better pipers than me, but the tunes were new to all of us, and over the last few years I had been used to much practice. Practice I did, because I wanted to be part of all this. I wanted to go 'over the top' with the rest of the lads.

Mr Percival would teach in the same manner as my old Pipey, in that he showed us how it should be done and how it should sound, leading by example, before analysing the written music manuscript.

I struggled at first, but Jock Percival was very patient and took time to coach each of us individually, as well as having us play as a group. 'Get it right, for God's sake, or you'll get a size nine up yer rectum' would be a popular encouragement. As the winter slowly passed, and that school may have looked like Disneyland but it certainly did not have the Florida heat, it all started to click. The Spring Term had arrived, and the Pipe Band was about to 'form up'. This apparently meant that the other lot down the hall, the Drummers, were about to grace us with their presence. I had quite forgotten about 'the other lot' as they were snobbishly referred to by us pipers, but then they are also unkindly known as 'Pipers Labourers'.

The drumming instructor was, I believe, an old police friend of Mr Percival and was very large and very jovial. Maybe, I thought, there must be less stress in teaching drumming than piping, but when the Head Drummer, or Drum Sergeant to give him his proper title, started fiddling about and generally being very impressive on the tappity tap front, I could see that they played their part on the team. It also meant that we got our pipes out for the first time in ages, having spent all winter on the chanter learning just three tunes.

There were knowing smiles all round from the Drum Corps, as us pipers huffed and puffed, totally out of blowing practice, trying to coordinate a simple tune like 'The Green Hills of Tyrol'. What a noise. We were all playing at different speeds and our pipes were all at different pitches. All in all, very humiliating, especially as the drummers were as tight as a Scotsman's wallet. As we collapsed, breathless, at the end of the session, the by now extremely jovial drum instructor shared a wink with Mr P and led his men off to their own room. We did not need reminding from Mr Percival, that there was work to be done before the summer, but that was the first game of the season, if you like, and we would only get better, surely.

We did get better, a lot better. Practice makes perfect, as they say, and once Mr Percival had fiddled with our pipe reeds, and sorted out our collective pipe noise so that we sounded as one, we started performing in earnest. The Fettes band now goes on tour in Hong Kong for a week, but in my day a gig at an old folks' home in Leith was as far as we got. That's probably why the band it is twice as big now. Incentive. I would even take up drumming if it got me to Hong Kong. The present-day Fettes band also have alternative, lightweight uniforms to wear for less formal occasions, or if the weather is hot. The summer of 1976 was hot all right. Believe me when I tell you, feeling the sweat dribbling down the inside of your thigh as you stride through 'Caber Feidh' wearing a kilt that feels like it is made out of an old duffel coat, and a tunic that was so heavy that it gradually bent its wire coat hanger within a week, is not a pleasant experience.

It is even worse in the rain. The whole get up doubles in weight so that your knees ache, and everyone smells like a damp dog. I mean the plaid alone, flying out behind you like a long tartan hearth rug absorbs water by the quart. But that's the Great Highland Bagpipe for you. At no time during any of this Pipes and Drums malarkey will anyone say that it's going to be easy, but hey, that's martyrdom for you. We suffer for our art.

Thoughts of this mere hindrance fly out of the window however, when you find out you are to play at Edinburgh Castle, in Scotland simply known as The Castle. Personally, I was most impressed at this new turn of events. What happens is that once a year, around May, all the Scottish Schools Pipe Bands get together and 'Beat the Retreat' on the castle Esplanade, the area in front of the castle gates. This is the place where they host the Tattoo, a huge extravaganza of music and displays from various cultures from around the world, as well as the obvious Scottish stuff, like pipe bands and highland dancing. I used to love the White Helmets, the Royal Signals motorcycle display team. I suppose like everyone else I was waiting for a mistake in the careful choreography to cause a gleeful smash up, but of course the Royal Signals bikers do not make mistakes. Anyway, the Tattoo is a major draw for the tourists during the Edinburgh Festival in August. We got to play there before any of the scaffolding and seating was put up, but crowds would be there just the same.

As with the sports field, a great rivalry exists between the bands, none more so when it became competition time in June. The Castle performance though was for the Good Stuff. Tunes made for marching, and for getting hairs on backs of necks to stand at attention. I was already familiar with most of the playlist, apart from a march called 'Dovecote Park' and a wonderfully named reel called 'Tail Toddle'. To this day I have no idea what it means, but it is a great wee tune to play, and I use it all the time.

We disembarked from the bus at our first 'massed' bands practice session at George Heriots' School one fine evening, to find other buses already disgorging their colourfully clothed youths, and unloading boxes of pipes, various shapes and sizes of drums, flight cases and other necessary equipment for a band on the road. Heriots was always used as the practice ground as it has a slightly sloping parade square out the back, not dissimilar to the slope at The Castle Esplanade itself. There was much adjusting of the leopard skin aprons as worn by bass and tenor drummers, dating back to the days when the superior African drummers of the British Army used them to protect their uniforms from the wear from their drums, banners bearing silk embroidered school crests for the Pipe Majors, fixing Glengarry, Balmoral or feather bonnet head-gear, and general hitching up of kilts or adjusting the drop of the sporran. Kilts do not travel well. I once wore one all the way to Chile on a plane, and what a state I arrived in.

All of a sudden, the all too familiar wheezy, screechy racket of all the pipers trying to 'tune up' assaulted the ears. The drummers calmly sat on their drum cases with an air of practiced indifference, examining their fingernails. Not for the first time would they subconsciously make the connection between that sound, and that of dragging nails down a blackboard. When all the instructors had had a quick cigarette and a gossip, for they knew each other well, and caught up from last year, it was time to 'form up' as one, massive Pipe Band. First up was good old rousing 'Highland Laddie', march past of the Black Watch, the London Scottish and the Scots Guards, and what a glorious hash up we made of it.

What had happened here was akin to the disaster that befell the Fettes band the day it had 'formed up', in that this time each band was playing at different speeds and pitches. The added spectacle of everyone marching out of time made the Dundee High School instructor gaze heavenwards, shaking his head, and Mr Percival examined something minute on his highly polished shoe. Some Heriots kids taking it all in while seated on a wall, were pointing and roaring with laughter. I laughed myself at the display, as did a few others, as the whole sorry mess dissolved into a kind of a halt, with the drummers all piling into each other at the back, as they had missed the signal to stop. A young piper, possibly from

Merchiston Castle School, was a full two bars behind everyone else at the end and received a friendly slap from his pal in the line for his trouble. All very amusing, and for once the seriousness attached to such matters had lessened, so we thought we would enjoy it while we could.

The instructors and the senior band members had seen it all before, however, and order was quickly restored for another crack at it, after some instrument maintenance, further tuning, and an angry conference between the Drum Sergeants. This time it was better but by no means perfect. The older, taller guys were reminded to take small steps going up the slope, so that the small people, like me, could keep up. Apparently one tiny drummer right at the very back, had given up playing and resorted to carrying his drum, and was moving along at a trot to keep up.

You will be surprised to hear me say this, but I have to admit I was having fun. If I had thought I was in a band before, well I was now in a Massed band. The Big Band.

Imagine being in the middle of nearly 100 pipers and the same number of drummers, and playing 'Highland Laddie' for all you're worth. It's a wall of sound. It is why, and I'm not joking about this, the Health and Safety say you have to wear ear plugs these days, although no one does. When you turn and 'counter march', which is when you turn at one end, and move back through the ranks that are still advancing, there is an odd phenomenon that occurs, which caught me off my guard, and put me in a mild panic. When you are moving through the other pipers, all you can hear are the other pipers, and that's good as you are all in synch. But here's the weird part. When you move through the drummers, all you can hear are the drums. No pipes, not even your own ones. It's the marching that keeps you in time.

Drummers have scant respect for discipline and decorum at the best of times, but as you are countermarching past the tenor drummers, they whack you on the side of your head with their fluffy ended sticks, which they twirl around all over the place. No one notices, and they will always claim after that it was an accident. It is stuff like this that is making the writing of this book so enjoyable, you would never know this if you have never been in a Pipe Band, and I love imparting the information.

At last it was C - Day. We boarded our bus with our gear with great solemnity and pride at what we were about to do, rather like it was the Memphis Belle's last flight, and tried not to scuff our white spats in the process. Oops, too late for me though, but after a withering look from our Pipe Major, who nodded at the Pipe Sergeant to get his Tippex bottle out of his sporran, we were all dressed up and ready to rock and roll.

At Heriots, when we formed up, we had all the space of their massive playground. Each school band would form one line astern, starting with the Pipe Major, obviously, then senior ranks, all the way down to the last in line of the pipers, me. After me the Drum Corps, resplendent in their red tunics as opposed to our blue ones, started with the Drum Sergeant and so on down the ranks. So that's fine and everyone knows their place. The drum majors are well out in front with their maces at the ready for the off. At The Castle, we could not form up on the actual Esplanade itself, because we had to enter on to it over the drawbridge, from behind the actual castle entrance.

On the other side of the drawbridge, away from the anticipation of the waiting crowds, there is absolutely no room whatsoever. If you have visited the place as a tourist, or even worked there as a soldier, you might find the space pleasant enough, but we are talking close to two hundred people crammed in here, all up against each other, with pointy drone things on their shoulders, and big drum things banging on their legs. I was interested to see how this was all going to work, and as if to answer my question, the Lead Drum Major called us all to order.

I will now at this point explain the role of the Drum Major. For a start he does not play any drums. He is the guy in the big hat, the Feathered Bonnet, who stands way out front from everyone else, and twirls about a long stick thingy, called a Mace. It is he who is responsible for the direction of travel of the band, and he does this with impressive movements of his mace, which to the band are interpreted as signals to stop, go, 'mark time' which is marching on the spot, wheel right, left and so on. The Pipe Major is in overall command of a band, but he can't shout out orders with a blowpipe stuck in his mouth. The Drum Major is therefore the figurehead, which is why he gets the big hat, the big stick, and usually the big ego to go with it.

"By the centerrrrrrrr..." came the order. "Quick march!" The drummers started their rolls and the Drum Majors turned on their heels and disappeared out over the drawbridge, as we struck up the first march, awkwardly marking time in that confined space to let them get ahead. Then the first two Pipe Majors of the first two bands moved out, their banners flying proudly, leading their swaggering men behind them. The drawbridge is only wide enough for two columns at a time, but soon it was our turn, there now being more people out on the Esplanade than there was back here. As we crossed out into that huge open space to line up with the other bands, who were all marking time to wait for us, I became aware of the crowds giving polite applause, and the odd cheer and whistle. Soon every band had 'formed up', and the Drum Majors raised their Maces to give the signal for the whole behemoth to lumber off down the slope.

It was always going to be alright on the night, and after forming a giant choreographed circle for the Strathspeys and Reels, we were brought to silence as the Drum Major of this year's Lead School strode up to the podium to ask permission of the General Officer Commanding, Scotland, to leave the field. This being granted, I had barely time to notice Captain Dad in the audience, straining for a view of little me in the middle of all this pageantry of flaming tartans, glittering silver and of course the terrible din, when we were off again. This time we filtered back through the Drawbridge to the strains of 'Scotland the Brave' and all bunched up ungainly as before, until the last man was over and we were signalled to stop, and then stood down.

I was able to have a quick chat with Dad before boarding the bus to take us home to school, and we both agreed that this day was something we could both be proud of. In the years to come I would make my way up the Fettes column until I stood at the very front, with my banner on, glaring menacingly at our own Drum Major. I can't wait to get to that story.

I know this has been a long chapter, but then a lot happened in this year. The Pipe Band Competition, hosted by Strathallan School up in Perthshire, was won by someone other than us, as usual, and I performed miserably in the Individual Section. On the way home in the coach Mr Percival seemed happy enough though, and pointed out that, at fourteen, I had a few years yet. Fair point that, and now the Summer Term was ending and it was time for everyone to go the other home, the one with the parents and the brothers and sisters in it.

None of this for me though, I had volunteered to go on the Cadet Force Summer Camp, and I couldn't wait! I watched all the big cars heading up the East Drive to pick up tearful offspring and indulge in a picnic out of the boot by the vast grassy lawns. No, my family had not seen me for so long, I reckoned they could just wait another week or two. I was packing all my Army kit methodically, like I was on a Special Mission, which I suppose I was, in a way. I had never been on a Camp before, but Gavin, my best pal back in Largo frequently went on the Scout ones, and seemed to enjoy them. He didn't get to wear camo cream on his face, or run through rivers with a gun though.

I had a suspicion that there were some kids on that camp who had been dumped there to give their parents one more week of freedom. They were certainly not as enthusiastic as me. One, in the Air Training Corps section, had not thought to draw boots from the stores, and promptly had his RAF shoe sucked off while marching across a muddy field. He had covered a good 20 yards before he had noticed. Someone gave him a glove to use on his foot till he got back to base.

Although I still had the lowly rank of Cadet, the appointment of Camp Piper afforded me some sort of status, in my eyes. Obviously, it was only because I was the only band member in attendance that year, but I would take on the job with the usual diligence and seriousness, as is the religion of the Bagpipe.

This entailed waking everyone up at six in the morning with a 'lively ditty' as the Camp Commanding Officer put it, of my own persuasion, although the Army will usually insist on 'Johnny Cope' as the standard Reveille tune. You can see what is coming here. If ever there was a more appalling and brutal way to be gently and delicately awakened from one's slumbers, this was it. I had made myself a target for an assorted range of make shift weapons to be found close to hand in a large six man tent, such as boots, training shoes, mess tins, the odd golf ball and the other RAF shoe. I nearly fell into the ditch that served as the camp latrine to avoid a well-aimed, wildly spinning, cricket bat.

The next morning, I cautiously struck up a little further away from the snoring circle of tents, but they had pre-empted me, and some bastard took a shot at me with an air pistol. Well, that was it. I stormed into the Officers' tent, threw my pipes on the floor, and announced that I was having no more of this insulting and abusive treatment. It was becoming dangerous. No one admitted to taking the shot, but I was replaced, along with my instrument, by a combination of a Corporal rattling a large saucepan with a heavy ladle; the idea being he could defend himself with the pan and hit back with the ladle.

I greatly enjoyed the Summer Camp after that, and even started to toy with the idea of joining the Army after leaving school, but then maybe the soldiers there are woken each morning by the sound of the Pipes, so maybe not. Let's face it I get enough of them as it is, with Mr Percival already unveiling the three new tunes for next year's competition. One day during the summer holidays, Dad and I went to visit Pipey in the big old house in St. Andrews, and Dad sat content with Bracken the dog in an armchair, while us two Pipers, the old and the young, marched round the big dining room table playing 'Men of Argyll' so that I could show off my new skills, and then 'Major Norman Orr Ewing' for old times' sake.

Chapter 6. Smoke on the water

*"Music is what tells us that the human race is
greater than we realise."*

Napoleon Bonaparte

The first top two places in the Combined Cadet Force NCO Cadre, which I had volunteered for, are appointed full Corporal rank. I came second, so I was jauntily off to visit the Sergeant Major in the stores to hand in one Doublet Ceremonial and pick up another, that of Pipe Corporal, which had two whole silver stripes on the upper sleeve. I also collected my new battledress armband which in addition to the stripes, had my Proficiency Star and Marksman badge sewn on. This trip was not nearly so intimidating as the last, as the Sergeant Major had been my instructor on the course, and as such was responsible for awarding me my marks. He did not exactly smile as he handed me my new kit over the counter, but there was a growing respect between us. I was fifteen years old now, I out-ranked some people in the Band older and more experienced than me, and was a veritable veteran of all things Band, and of Cadets. I was no longer the new guy in town, and I was going places.

The next year's routine was no different, and another set of tunes were already being learnt over the winter for the June competition. Now that I had reached the level of the rank and prestige that is Pipe Corporal, the old bear that is a Burns Supper was rearing its ugly head once more. People in Edinburgh found it quite convenient to telephone a school such as Fettes, to provide them with the requisite Piper for their bashes, and they all happen more or less around the same day, 25th January, the great man's birthday. Demand was usually high, and once our Pipe Major had bagged all the best ones, meaning the ones with the most free booze, the Pipe Sergeant had the pick of the rest, and, as next in line, I was left with the Temperance Society of the Free Kirk Masonic Abstinence branch of Alcoholics Anonymous.

Not that we were allowed to drink alcohol, of course, being under age for one, but, you see, it is tradition. We all by now know of this tradition, ceremony, and indeed religion almost, that is the Highland Bagpipe. Assuming you arrive there in one piece at the Top Table, The Piper must toast the Queen in the appropriate manner, in Gaelic, which translates as 'King Woman', as that language does not possess a word for 'Queen' in its vocabulary. Gaelic is an old and noble language, from the days when queens were not trusted to do the business with the Big Sword on the battlefield, so they simply did not have any. Only kings and their wives. It is a language I have a great respect for, and absolutely no desire to learn whatsoever, as all my friends speak English, even the American ones. The Jardine clan motto, incidentally, is 'Cave Adsum', or 'Beware, I Am Here', and that's Latin.

I had, for a laugh, felt like announcing in a loud voice: 'Beware! I Am Here!' to the lovely old ladies at the Morningside Guild of Retired Tapestry Weavers, whose Burns Night do had been only the night before, but in tonight's company, maybe not a good idea. This was some rugby club or other, and it had been a last-minute thing as the Pipe Major had flu apparently. I had been dropped off at the club door by a teacher in his car, and not wanting to pop in 'for a wee dram', he left me with instructions to make my own way home in a taxi, and was off.

These men knew how to party, and much merriment was being had by some big bloke pouring some concoction down another big bloke's throat, to some sort of Aboriginal chant, from what I could make out. I felt slightly out of my depth, but I was a soldier, and a Full Corporal to boot, and not a cowering wee ten-year-old in a steamy kitchen in Elie. I did wonder however, what our boss, the Pipe Major, or even the Pipe Sergeant, a keen rugby player himself, would have made of it. The realisation was beginning to dawn on me, that these guys had turned this gig down. I had been set up.

It was utter carnage in the kitchen, with everyone pitching in as to how much Drambuie to pour into the Atholl Brose desert, and by the looks of things, it was by now looking rather watered down. As if to compensate, some drunk with Saltire boxer shorts on his head, was attempting to drain the excess fluid with a ladle, and tipping the contents into the mashed neeps, after a quick swig himself. At this point in my life I was unacquainted with the effects of alcohol, and these days we are all aware of the need for moderation, but had it been a few years down the line, I would have been taking a gulp from the Drambuie bottle myself at this point, for courage.

There was lots of back slapping and hugging going on, and there was always the mysterious Aboriginal chant thing going on in the background. Or foreground, as suddenly some sort of conga like procession swung in through the kitchen doors. "Oh, we've got a Piper, Oh we've got a Piper, ta ra ra rah, ta ra ra rah!". God knows what state the food was in by now, but the boys wanted their scoff, and they wanted it "Now, Now, Now!"

Without further ado, the appointed Bearer of the Haggis was duly found under a chair, woken up, slapped about a bit, and given a shot of tequila to sober him up. Game On once more, and I swear I could not hear myself play, and that's saying something with the Pipes, as the cheers went up at the entrance of the hallowed Grub for the Lads, "Bring it on, bring it on!" Lots of pig grunting sounds now replaced the Aboriginal chant, and I strained my peripheral vision to see if the pissed guy was still behind me, or had already lobbed the salver of haggis over the head of some poor punter at the table.

He was being supported, or rather steered, by two mates, that were as equally inebriated, but they doggedly kept up with me as I swept along, my marching and deportment ruggedly intact, as always. A very large man in a bow tie, who was sweating profusely, grandly accepted the Haggis as it was placed, but oh so nearly tipped, onto the High Table. I was rigid at attention, as I should be at this moment, to the right of the person at The High Table, who would give the Address to the Haggis.

Why this foul smelling and awful tasting 'delicacy' should be accorded an address is beyond me, but that is the Scottish Way. Tradition. Through all this haze of debauchery, I drift off in a daydream, and remember my parents forcing me to watch these appalling television shows in the 1970s, because it was Scottish, with men in pink tartan kilts singing ballads about roses, or kisses, with bouffant hair. "It's yer heritage, so you'll like it!" I remember the studio audience would be sitting around on bales of straw, clapping away as the girls did their dance routines, holding up the edges of their skirts as they wove around some bloke with an accordion. Believe it or not I have actually appeared in a Peter Morrison music video as the 'Rogue Piper O' Dundee', and if anyone comes across it let me have a copy, as I lost mine years ago. The part where I wink at the camera at the end, in slow motion, is cringingly hilarious.

Back to reality now, and it is Time for 'The Toast to The Queen'. Silence and great solemnity descends, and I swear there was a big man crying somewhere, as I gave The Toast: "Slange va ban Riach". I know that's not how it's written but that's how it sounds, before anyone complains. I am then presented with a '*quaich*', which is a small silver bowl with two handles on either side, usually commemorative in some sort of way. I then raise it to my lips with a flourish, to drain the contents in one, like I had seen in Western movies.

I don't know what they put in the whisky bottles in the movies, but the *quaich* was full to the brim with the real stuff. I had watched them sloshing it in, the bottle bearing the legend 'Ardbeg Twelve-Year-Old'. I had not drunk whisky before, but at fifteen I felt almost a man, so how hard would it be? This particular *quaich* was the size of a Great Dane's dog bowl, and overflowing with the amber nectar. I downed it, but it took me three gulps. Job done, I struck up the Pipes, resolved to play 'Black Bear' and then set off back out of the room, as an unwelcome feeling started to well up in my stomach. The Whisky, it would seem, did not like it down there and wanted out, and it wanted out now. I had to speed things up a bit or there may be a disaster. The clapping now accelerated up in to a form of an applause, as the crowd tried to keep up with the tune. I hurtled toward the sanctuary of the kitchen, which seemed a mile away. 'Black Bear' is a very fast tune to play, as per beats per minute, in its proper form, but I had no time for proper anything now. I remember being impressed with myself at the time, for not fluffing a single note, as I played the venerable March Past of the Argylls faster and faster, until mercifully I clattered through the sanctuary of the swing doors.

My mouth was under the cold water tap within seconds, pipes still on my shoulder, and after many gulps the situation appeared to be resolved, and I felt very happy. So happy in fact, that I hugged the chef, and helped myself to some alcoholic neeps. This wasn't so bad, I reasoned. At least I did not have to sit through all the boring stuff, as it was an in and out job. An 'in and out jobbie', ha, ha! I thought this remark extremely funny, and began to tell all and sundry, all the while losing some vision in my left eye. This was in turn was causing some confusion in the part of my brain which controlled balance, and I kept veering to the right. After a few minutes of starboard circling, like I was a battleship whose rudder has been blown off by a torpedo, it was clear that I needed to get home, and soon.

As I staggered off at a slight tilt to one side, I wondered why the weight of my pipe box had never been a cause for concern before. A club member's wife kindly offered to give me a lift back to my school. "Shanks, I'm f-f fine," I dribbled out of my slack jaw. She insisted, however, as it was on her way home with her comatose husband. Gratefully, after some difficulty extracting myself from her tiny car, I slammed the car door shut at the school gates, and whacked the roof twice with my hand to show my appreciation. Then I opened the door again to free my plaid, half of which was still in the back seat, and then lurched in the general direction of School House West and my dormitory. I did not know what time it was but suddenly I had an overwhelming desire to go to sleep. Maybe in those nice bushes over there, beside the entrance to the Dining Hall, I thought. Instinct, however, told me that I must make it to my dorm, for fear of repercussions the next morning, and because it was starting to rain.

I commandeered two bemused –and indeed amused- juniors to act as crutches to get me up the stone spiral staircase, and I bade them a merry farewell at the door of the dorm. Luckily there was no one else in the room, as I attempted to take my uniform off in totally the wrong order. I began to unbutton my tunic, and tried to haul it off from under the tightly wrapped plaid, but gave that up after a while. I then successfully managed to take off my kilt, from under my sporran, but I left it at one shoe and spat off, after falling forward and head-butting my chest of drawers in the removal process. I was by now quite exhausted, and so, satisfied that I had done my best under the circumstances, and with a quiet giggle, I climbed into bed and oblivion.

Watching *Top of the Pops* or listening to Radio 1 at home in Largo during the holidays, was pretty much my music scene back then, and Radio Luxembourg if one was feeling exotic. The pop singles charts in the mid-1970s was dire anyway, the glam of T. Rex and Bowie being replaced by the disco of Saturday Night Fever. I never knew, until a knowledgeable friend of mine played it to me on a cassette player, there was such a thing as Heavy Rock. This was indeed a revelation, and I was hooked instantly. Deep Purple were one of my favourites, but unfortunately they had split up in 1974. Not to worry though as my learned friend told me of the offshoots that had followed, most notably Ritchie Blackmore's Rainbow and Whitesnake.

These songs did not fade away at the end with a whimper, but finished with a bang of joyful noise, and clashes of symbols, like a Beethoven concerto. And, like the classical violinist or pianist, there was impressive technical musicianship in there. The mists were beginning to clear. At last, here was an instrument that I actually wanted to play. An instrument capable of such power, but also of delicate subtlety. A most versatile thing that could make all sorts of different sounds, and provoke all kinds of emotions. It was beautiful, and I wanted to reach out and caress it, to run my hand over its sensual curves. It was the Electric Guitar.

Our new Pipe Major was a cool dude, someone I knew well as he was also in my House. He was from Blair Atholl and played for the Vale of Atholl Pipe Band in the holidays, and secretly had a motorbike stashed somewhere over in the Western General Hospital. His name was Funky Adams, and he played guitar.

I could not believe it! How could he play pipes *and* guitar? I have told in graphic and gory detail of my experiences and frustrations learning and practising bagpipes. I could not possibly go through all that again with a new instrument, although, for love, I might be willing to make the sacrifice. Apparently, my guitar hero Ritchie Blackmore practiced eight hours a day, which was fine, but he did not have classes and homework and the like. Also, I was fairly certain he did not have to play in a Pipe Band either.

It had been one evening that I popped up to the sixth form study/bedrooms to speak to Funky about Band matters. As I walked along the corridor to his room, I could hear the sound of an electric guitar. The tone set up was beefy, with some mild distortion and a hint of reverb. Marcus 'Funky' Adams was sat on the edge of his bed playing an improvised solo, that is to say, anything that comes in to your head. The complete opposite, in fact, of the rigidity that is The Scots Guards Standard Settings.

"Hi, there!" greeted Funky cheerily. "Want a shot?" Whoa, this was a shock. "I can't... I mean I don't know how," I stammered, as I backed away nervously from the proffered instrument, which had started to feedback with a faint whine, like a baby when taken out of its mother's arms. "It's easy," said Funky. "I'll show you." With that, he gathered his baby close to him once more, and proceeded to play the opening chords to 'Smoke on the Water', a Deep Purple classic. A progression of four simple chords played on just two strings. Easy peasy. This song turned out to be the guitar equivalent to good old 'Scots Wha' Hae', and a great training device for the aspiring Rock God.

All of a sudden, it was as if I was back in some sort of time warp. Funky had the guitar plastered all over me in an instant, the strap over my shoulder, a pick in my fingers, and the familiar coaxing of "Get your elbow further round, like that" or "No, try to keep this wrist bent, and these fingers straight" and "Relax, mate, you don't want to play guitar standing to attention. Go on, strike a pose! Knock yourself out!"

With a giddying sense of 'déjà vu', Funky had decided that we had had enough fun for one day, and unplugged various leads, and switched off knobs on the amplifier. I went back to my study all wide-eyed and excited, to tell my studymates what had just occurred. I had actually played an electric guitar! It transpired that Funky was so nick named by his peers because of his very un-Public School flair for playing a 'cool' instrument, the norm back in those days being French horns, church organs and the like. And he even played in a Rock Band. He explained that having learnt to play the bagpipes meant I would pick up guitar quickly, no problem, or indeed any other instrument, as my fingers and brain were used to moving fast, and also because other instruments by comparison were so much easier to learn.

Important news indeed, to be filed away for future reference. But this book is about The Pipes, and to get back on track, Pipe Major 'Funky' Adams and I, along with the rest of the Band, were soon labouring away with our new set of tunes for the coming year. I had suggested 'Wullie Cumming's Rant' for our Reel, just because of the great name. I mean who or what on God's earth had rattled Wullie's cage so much that the ensuing rant would be commemorated by a pipe tune, in the same way that the '79th Farewell to Gibralter' was similarly immortalised. I wonder if there may be some information somewhere, of what it was that Wullie was so worked up about, so I can pick up a few tips.

Mr. P had other more ambitious plans however. I think our Strathspey that year may well have been 'The Caledonian Canal' but I have no idea about the rest, only that they were damned difficult, and sounded incredibly boring. Playing 'The Caledonian Canal' is like wading through the actual canal itself. Anyway, it was nothing the Fettes College Pipes and Drums boys couldn't handle, and this year we were determined to win. Even third would do, actually, so we could take home a medal for once. So we applied ourselves to the job in hand, for We Were Pipers (and Drummers), and proud of it. We just needed to keep our rectums a keen distance from Mr. Percival's size nines.

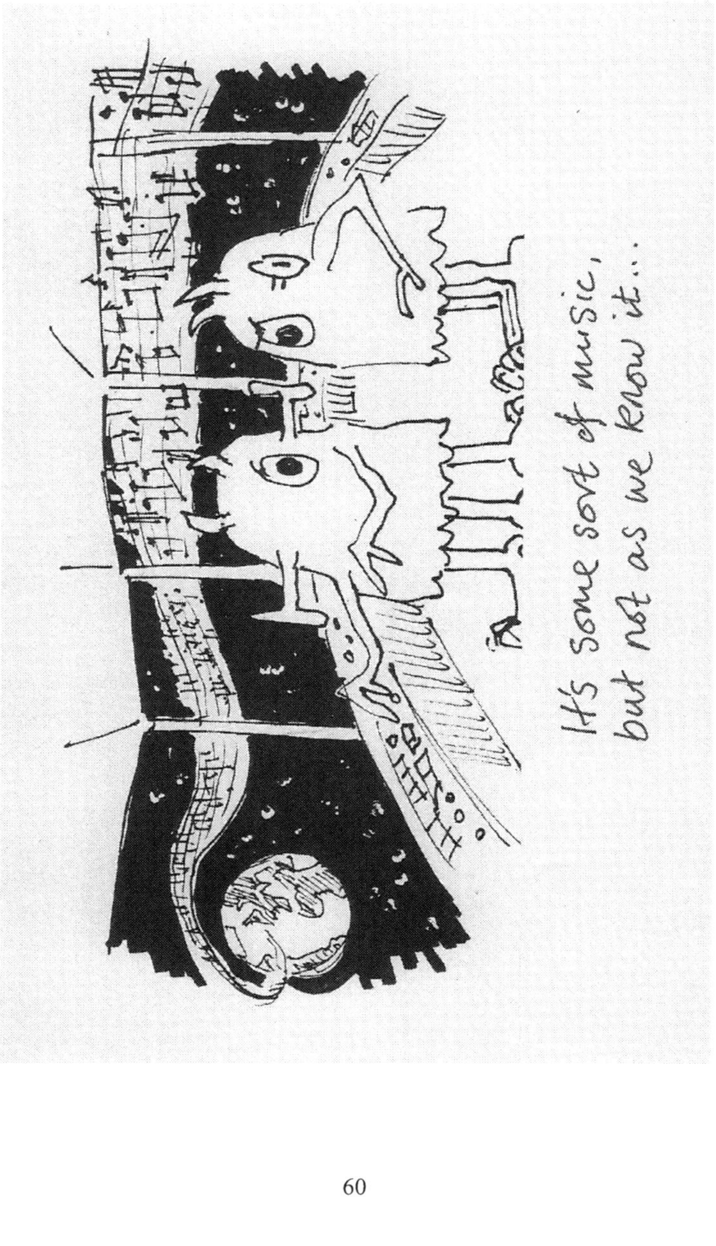
It's some sort of music,
but not as we know it...

Chapter 7. Tossers and soggy banners

"If the Scottish want to break away, I shall stand on Hadrian's Wall with a teary handkerchief and say 'Good riddance to the lot of you, and take your stupid bagpipes with you!'"

Jeremy Clarkson

The summer drew to a close with no medals again for the Pipes and Drums in the annual Schools Competition, although I did not fair too badly in the individual events.

It was not the case that we were not a good Pipe Band, but just that everyone else seemed to be better than us on the day. It was much the same scenario with the Scotland football team, who had shown so much promise in the qualifying rounds for the 1978 World Cup in Argentina, only to snatch defeat from the jaws of victory yet again. There was one fan, apparently, who had left his wife, kids, and job, to travel to South America, and was too ashamed to return. He hitch-hiked up to Canada where he still lives, working as a carpenter.

Considering that we are a small nation of five million souls, compared to, say, England's sixty million, I don't think that we do too badly. The Scottish game, it is said in some in pubs up and down the country, that we may lack the finesse of the Brazilians, or the Italians. Or of the French or the Germans, and that is where we are going wrong. I have a theory about this, which I know you would love to share with me, and yes, you guessed it, it all goes back to Tradition.

Two words then: Highland Games. Scotland's traditional sporting events. These are played out in a large field somewhere near small villages all over the country, every summer. Once the cows have been cleared away, and most of the cow crap, the all-important and indeed focus point, marquee is set up in the middle. This large tent is known as the Beer Tent, and this is where you will head for as soon as you arrive, to prepare you for a day of truly unrivalled sporting entertainment.

These events are essentially an excuse for a spectacular piss up, by both spectators and performers, sorry 'sportsmen', alike, so one has to try and keep one's wits about a person in case you have to unavoidably step in a reasonably fresh cow pat, whilst moving to avoid a miss thrown Ball and Chain. All around, in various roped off enclosures, very large people, usually men, will be enthralling spectators by huffing and puffing while attempting to do things involving various heavy objects. All this while attempting to win a secondary and parallel competition, to see who can pull the most ugly and contorted face.

There is the 'Hammer Throwing' which consists of, er, lobbing a sledge hammer at some judges who are anxiously holding a tape measure; 'Boulder Lifting' where a big man will attempt to mate with a large boulder before hoisting it above his head in triumph, and 'Throwing A Rock At Your Pal's Head', which is fairly self-explanatory. All this to great roars of appreciation from the crowds, usually attired in kilts, but with large boots and rolled down socks, so as not to ruin one's good brogue shoes in the cow shit. This is the fashion of course, adopted by Scotland rugby supporters, which says it all. Incidentally the 'sportsmen' do not appear to wear sporrans with their kilts. Maybe they are worn underneath to keep them out of the way.

There are of course some running events and the like, but there is always the risk of a twisted ankle due to the uneven ground, and so for health and safety reasons, running is done while in a sack. Old grain ones are said to be the best. My favourite Traditional Scottish Sport is where a big bloke picks up an entire telegraph pole by its base, and heaves it into the air with a loud grunt, coupled with the sort of rasping fart which sounds like it must have hurt. This 'sport' is called 'Tossing the Caber', origins of which go back to when a makeshift bridge was needed over a stretch of river, and a handy tree trunk or two was lobbed across with great accuracy and power. If you want a laugh, go up to one of these guys in the beer tent and ask him if he is a caber tosser, then watch as the Neanderthal features try to figure out if this might be a compliment or offering insult.

Just to emphasize the Scottishness of it all, there is always a Pipe Band at these events, usually completely legless, having been topping up their cans of McEwan's Export from the beer tent with whisky from ergonomically designed sporran flasks. The sound is always appalling but no one notices anyway. Indeed, as a handful of out of tune and out of time pipers and drummers stagger around the field, there is often to be heard the odd slurred comment, such as 'Aye, man. Ye cannae beat the sound o' the Pipes!' Really? At a Highland Games? I beg to differ.

I will never forget the time at the Ceres Games in Fife, when a side drummer - they're the ones that make the rattle sound - took umbrage to the fact that a tenor drummer, a 'thumper', had inadvertently caught him in the face with his fluffy stick, while aiming for a junior piper. The resultant attempt to poke the man in the eye with his own, pointy, stick, led to a riot within the band ranks. There are only three policemen stationed in nearby Cupar, who take turns to work in shifts, so the sole copper on duty had to call in a van load from Dundee to sort it out, by which time women were ripping each other's shirts off, the beer tent was listing drunkenly to one side, and the Drum Major had had his big Feathered Bonnet flattened by someone with his own mace.

The highlight at the end of the day at any games though, is the 'Tug O' War'. The women gather up the children and hasten home to board up the windows, and bring in the dog, as two teams of the Biggest of the Big gather menacingly around an innocuous length of thick rope. The complex rules of this game are thus: the rope will be pulled in opposite directions by the two teams, until the centre of the rope crosses over a line. Got that? Good. Usually there will be some rivalry in there, such as two different pubs, or two different families even. One thing is for sure, each team will take this last 'sporting' event of the day very seriously indeed.

The two teams take the strain, legs apart, knees in the air, like a long line of women in birthing chairs, their faces writhed in agony for that last, final, push. Or in this case pull of course. But now it's all over, and let the brawl commence as the accusations of cheating fly. In this case there had been a late addition of a 'ringer' in the form of a twenty stone Chicago policeman, who had been spotted in Ladybank on a golfing holiday with his wife, and had innocently agreed to 'help out' as it was 'all for charity' on the day. And so the supporters of the two teams piled in. And if you have a minor grievance with your neighbour, now is the time to pitch in and lamp him one, as all will be forgotten, and therefore forgiven, by the next day.

So, finesse, as I have illustrated, is not in the genetic make up of the Scottish sportsman. Indeed, it would appear that we are not very good at team sports in general. Think about it. We have good racing and rallying drivers, snooker, darts and golf players, and, although nobody ever notices, we always win the first Commonwealth Gold for Bowls. Or Target Shooting. Or even Grouse Hurling, or Caber Tossing. All individual sports, notice, so we must lump our football teams in with our Tug O' War teams in the 'could do better' categories.

It has to be said though, at a Highland Games the closest you will get to a team effort is, in fact, the Pipe Band. If you break up the sum of the parts, obviously the piper can stand alone, outside a church in the rain for instance, waiting for a wedding party. But what of the poor Bass Drummer? He could bang away on his own, giving it thump thump thump like a giant, muffled metronome, but what would be the point? If such a thing as a Roman slave galley was still in existence, he could get the job of keeping the rhythm of the rowers. There would be Sailing Speed (March), Battle Speed (Strathspey), moving up to Ramming Speed (Reel). And another thing. Has anyone ever wondered how, or if, these people practice?

I remember that at a recent World Pipe Band Championship, the prize for Best Bass Drummer went to a girl from Dysart and Dundonald Pipe Band. I often wonder how on earth they judge that? Do the judges have metronomes built into their mobile phones, to gauge the precision of the 'thump', and hand-held GPS systems to make sure that their dressing is correct within the band? Maybe they receive extra marks for accuracy and sly force exerted, for that clandestine whack in the face with a fluffy stick, of a junior piper on the counter march. Mockery apart, they are, however, part of the team.

Anyway, it was a new school year, and talking of teams brings me neatly on to the big news in my world of all things Pipe. I suppose I should have seen it coming, but it was still rather a shock all the same. I had joined our 'team', The Band, so young that there was now no one older than me that had my experience. There were older people in the band of course, but they had all joined after me. Arise, then, Pipe Major A. T. Jardine!

So apart from yet another jacket, this time with the four 'upside down' chevrons on the sleeve, and the red sash worn by senior NCO rank of sergeant and above, oh, and the School Banner, the really cool thing about this was as Pipe Major I out-ranked all the other sergeants in our entire Cadet Force. I would even out-rank the Sergeant who was captain of our Shooting Team, of which I was a part, though he was still the boss and would go up to collect any prizes we won, which wasn't as often as I would have liked. The Edinburgh

Academy 1st VIII in those days were to the Target Rifle what The Brothers of Prestonpans were to the Highland Bagpipe. We shared a coach with them when we went off to competitions, even as far as Bisley outside London, and a great bunch of lads they were. Their laid back, shirt tails out, hands in pockets attitude was perfectly suited to the mental discipline of target shooting. They were so laid back in fact, that it was said that they could slow their pulse rates down to almost zero. Consequently, they never missed.

But I digress once more. One day the Commanding Officer of Fettes College Combined Cadet Force called me in to his office for a chat. His name was Colonel Hills, an affable man who at one point was also my maths teacher. After congratulating me on my appointment, he began to make it clear that he was expecting great things from both me, and from the band this year. A previously unknown feeling, that of responsibility, was starting to hang about me like a wet plaid.

My promotion to Pipe Major, still only at the age of sixteen, had come at a price. A raft of talented pipers, like Funky Adams, were all two years above me, and had now left the school. Much work had to be done, and I was now the Boss Man, the Big Cheese as it were, and as such discipline would have to be maintained.

I had no problems with the older guys, as they accepted that I was more experienced, and probably the better piper, but it was the ones my own age. They simply took the piss. Of course, the drummers were the worst. One great wheeze was to simply keep going in the same direction at the counter march, instead of turning around to follow the pipers. As the drummers were behind us, we pipers would be unaware of this, and it would be a bemused bunch of pensioners in Leith, who witnessed both halves of the band moving apart in opposite directions.

Another would be the bass and tenor drummers - the happy thumpers - would hit an 'off' beat, rather than hit in time to the foot hitting the ground. This jazz effect did make everything sound hilariously ridiculous, to me also, but eventually everything would fall apart with the pipers spluttering and choking with laughter into their blowpipes, and the errant drummers giggling like naughty schoolgirls as they abandoned their drums and ran for it before I could get my hands round their throats. Happy days.

Slowly, as the year moved on, it all started coming together as usual, and the annual Beating of the Retreat at Edinburgh Castle was upon us once more, and this year, wait for it, we were to be the Lead Band! I loved the Castle gig, but all of a sudden, I yearned for the days when I was at the back of the line, not a care in the world but to enjoy the occasion, and ducking the odd fluffy drumstick being my only stress.

But no, this year I was to be not only at the front, but first out over that historic drawbridge as well. Now, remember the shock I felt when I first discovered that when counter marching through the lines of drummers, all you hear are the drummers? Well even at my relatively tender years I thought I had seen and heard it all. Bear with me while I explain.

Only two lines can fit over the bridge at a time, and no one told me that once over that drawbridge, everything stops. Literally. Even Time itself. Everyone else is still behind the walls so all I could hear was me and the Pipe Major from Stewart's Melville College alongside. No rest of the pipers, no drummers rattling, no thumpers thumping, no crunch of Army issue brogue on cobble. I couldn't see anyone and I couldn't hear anyone. Before I had time to properly panic though, the Drum Majors, who had gone ahead, had turned and raised their maces parallel to the ground with both arms, the signal to 'mark time' which is sort of marching on the spot. Slowly the lines of the other bands were starting to make their crossings, and were drawing up alongside, bringing with them, louder and louder, the good old familiar, fantastic din that is a Massed Band at full tilt.

Once fully assembled, like one of these Roman fighting formations, the whole behemoth lumbers off, a proud Pipe

Major at the head of each line, at the head of his band, leading his bandmates onwards, kilts swinging, the School Crest on the School Banner fluttering from the bass drone in the summer breeze. The Drum Majors in their big hats, were twirling expertly their gleaming maces in their immaculate white gloves. It doesn't get any better than this.

On this day it was bucketing rain. We were all crammed together once again on the Castle side of the drawbridge, waiting for the signal to strike up. Everyone was slightly grumpy, and I don't think the Heriots Pipe Major was too impressed with the way the Highland Broadsword that I was wearing from dear old Pipey's swag cupboard, kept jabbing him in the knee. Pipe Major Barron had surprised me by turning up with a car boot full of priceless antiques for me to carry for the occasion. Apart from the sword, there was a handsome bejewelled dirk, which is a long knife worn at the side, his own priceless *sgian dubh*, grouse cock feathers for my Glengarry hat, and a plaid brooch with an inlaid gem stone that looked like a brother to the Star of India. I felt, literally, like a million dollars, but I could hear some discussion over my shoulder as to whether the Pipe Majors should remove their banners, for fear that the waterlogged cloth might have the serious consequence of snapping the bass drone to which they are attached.

Before any of this rumbling dissent went any further, I squeezed round as best I could, giving the Watsons' Drum Major an eye watering poke in the sporran with Pipey's sword, and reminded the assembled and distinguished company, that as Fettes were Lead Band, I was in overall charge, and that if anyone wished to remove their soggy banners, then fine, but I'm first out, my dad and my old instructor are here to watch, I'm wearing an antique sword, and my banner stays on.

I was a bit flushed after that, but to a man, they all left them on, and there were no calamities in the drone snapping department. As our Drum Major halted at the podium with his usual flourish, to ask permission to leave the parade, I spotted the Captain and the Pipe Major in the audience. They had come to witness the fruit of their labours at first hand, at the head of hundreds of Pipers and Drummers at Edinburgh Castle. I'll never forget that moment.

Then it was 'Scotland the Brave', and back up through the Drawbridge for another year.

Who's making that terrible noise?

Chapter 8. Hotel California

Here's to it;
The fighting sheen of it;
The yellow, the green of it;
The white, the blue of it;
The dark, the red of it;
Every thread of it;
The fair have sighed for it;
The brave have died for it;
Honour the name of it;
Drink to the fame of it –
The Tartan!

Murdoch Maclean

I always love wearing the kilt. Note that I say *the* kilt and not *a* kilt. Of course, as I write this I am lounging in my customary jeans and T-shirt, and that's a good thing. When one needs to dress up for an occasion, then the ubiquitous suit can make one feel as if some sort of effort has been made, including ironing a shirt and polishing 'proper' shoes, that sort of thing. Work wear should be exactly that, casual clothes that are comfortable and practical in the workplace whether it's the head office of the Bank of England or the Antarctic Survey Station at the South Pole.

The kilt has special reverence in Scotland. It is acknowledged around the world as the national dress of the country as Bagpipes are to be the national instrument, so naturally the two go together. I was in Seoul, South Korea a few years ago, doing a spot of piping at the VisitScotland stand at a travel fair, like you do. The puppeteers of the Bulgarian stand next door would become most perturbed when I gave them a blast in the middle of their performance, but once we sorted out some sort of rhythm, mutual appreciation was acquired and they let me share the stash of beer they had hidden under their little stage. After a while I stepped out to get away from the endless selfie phone photo poses, and of having to take my pipes to bits to show them where all the racket came from. I dodged the traffic, running in all my finery to a bar across the street from the conference centre, and pushed through the hanging door netting, getting a strand caught up in my medals in the process. After a cursory glance in my direction, and accepting the fact it would appear that a Scotsman had come among them, the drinkers simply got back to their business and ignored me. Eight time zones away and these people knew exactly what I was.

We here in Scotland do not wear kilts very often. It is reserved for the most special of occasions like Hogmanay, Scotland v England rugby matches, and the odd wedding. But when that nearly two yards of tartan cloth is strapped on, it is said that a man becomes a 'man and a half'. There feels a need to stand tall and proud. There are no pockets so arms swing when marching, the military heritage seeping through. No slouching when seated either, in case of exposure of The Secret, so one is constantly at attention. Head held high and with movement, the swagger initiates the kilt pleats at the back to sashay back and forth, creating the famous 'swing' of the kilt. Women admire and envy a man in a kilt, for they cannot get a skirt to swing in the same way. Something to do with the more Neanderthal physique of the male hips, so I'm told.

The colourful vertical and horizontal check patterns woven into the cloth of a kilt are known as tartan. Each Scottish clan has its own design, and these are proudly worn by individuals whose families have an affiliation with or connection to a clan, and quite rightly so. The Royal Navy's recently commissioned Type 45 Destroyer HMS Duncan for instance, has Blue Duncan tartan upholstery throughout. And Rod Stewart, the old dog, is so proud of his Scottish roots that he has his band's drumkit kitted out in the gaudy bright red Royal Stewart tartan, not to mention the bass drum skin embellished with the crest of Celtic Football Club, football in this country being another example of sometimes fanatical tribal pride. If I was his drummer, I might have something to say about this, but no matter. There are no hard and fast rules, so if you happen to be enamoured by the soft lilac hues of Rutherford for instance, feel free to order a bolt or two for your kilt, ballgown, car seat covers, cycling shorts and living room curtains if you like.

Tartans, like most things Scottish these days, are everywhere, but it was never always the case. In the old days, tribes of the peoples of the Highlands of Scotland wore large wrap around garments that doubled up as a tent and blanket for when the wind got up, and it was too late to make it home to the cosy, peat fired bothy in the settlement. The wool fabric was dyed with whatever came to hand to waterproof it, I dread to think what, and the patterns and hues produced were always a bit different from that lot along the glen, giving the wearer some sense of identity.

But then some significant historical events were to change everything. After the last of the Jacobite independence uprisings was quelled in the mid-18th century, a few laws were introduced, for instance banning weapons, including the bagpipes, north of the border apart from military personnel, and not just to piss them off, but more to keep that rebellious Highland identity in check, even making the wearing of anything tartan illegal. Then one day, King George IV (of Scotland and England) decided to visit Edinburgh in 1822, the first visit to Scotland by a reigning monarch in two centuries. This was a most important occasion indeed to the more 'civilised' Lowland parts of Scotland, and so the esteemed novelist Sir Walter Scott was put in charge of the appropriate preparations to be made.

What he did was an astounding gamble. Not only were the decorations and the assembled dignitaries got up in the finest tartans, but he even persuaded the King himself to be swathed in the cloth of the Clans, and he enjoyed it all immensely. Instantly, with this apparent Royal approval, the rebellious tartan was fashionable the length of the land and beyond. Brighter colours that were now available from trade across the world like the admired reds, yellows, greens and blues of silks from India and the Orient were seen as the way forward.

Sensing an opportunity, weavers got to work immediately. At Highland games and other gatherings, clan chiefs wanted to wear their own Clan Tartan so the weavers simply invented them. The Scots boss of a plantation overseas wanted all of his two hundred (quite possibly slave) workers sporting his family colours of MacIntyre and was happy to receive a good deal on two hundred aprons of what we would now call Melville, but no one was any the wiser and so no one cared. The weavers simply had a surplus of what they were punting as Melville in stock. These days it's all more controlled, and apart from the old traditional family and Regimental tartans, new ones can be created if there's a valid enough reason – even some football clubs have them – but strictly subject to the approval of course, of The Scottish Register of Tartans.

Next came the re-design of the kilt as we know it today, and hold on to your sporran here, as it amuses me to tell you that...

It was invented by an Englishman.

He was a man named Thomas Rawlinson, who had large mills of the sort all over England during the Industrial Revolution, and families to fill the vast production lines were brought in from the Highlands of Scotland, who, having lost their livings from farming crofts to aggressive English and Lowland sheep rearing landowners, were grateful of the work. Their long wrap around costumes of fabric were known as the Great Kilt, and held all together with one simple large pin, removal of which would render the wearer naked.

Being cumbersome in a battle the garment could be easily discarded before a great Highland Charge, and for historical accuracy and better spectacle I'd like to see Mel Gibson careering down the hill at Falkirk with his accompanying rabble in nothing but their under-shirts or as was more likely, in nothing at all. It is still retained symbolically in the modern Pipers Plaid, held in place by a decorative brooch but needing some assistance to put on. The wearer of a Great Kilt simply spreads the thing on the ground, lays down and rolls up in it.

Being a man with an early perspective of Health and Safety, Rawlinson saw the need for a simpler garment that would not keep becoming tangled in the machinery, inconveniently reducing his workforce by loss of limb or worse, and being inspired by the practicality of the Roman soldiers fighting 'skirt', the kilt, as we know it today, was born.

Fettes College wears the dark green and blue with thin red and yellow stripes of Hunting Stewart, the tartan worn by our affiliated regiment The Royal Scots, the oldest regiment in the British Army, now part of 1st Battalion Royal Regiment of Scotland, recruiting from Edinburgh and the Borders, and we came second, second d'you hear, at the Scottish Schools Pipe Band Championship in the summer of 1980. Our Drum Major, Nick Urquhart, strode purposefully up to the podium to collect our cup and medals, and came to the halt, with his usual flourish, which I am sure was becoming more and more flourishable lately, if that's a word, then threw a perfect salute. I had grown up with Nick and knew him well, and I reckon he was maybe, mischievously, attempting to expose The Secret to the assembled throng, albeit for a laugh, and in the strict military manner of the Halt.

Recently Nick's flourishing had achieved such heights, literally, that at the usual old folks' home bash he had, in a most cavalier fashion, lobbed his mace high up into the air only for it to land upright, stuck in the grass, shivering with fright, a good 30 yards in front of him. Of course, he just marched past it and simply plucked it from the ground, with a flourish, and subsequently refused to entertain any notion whatsoever that the whole stunt was not done on purpose.

It was the time of year again for the Beating of the Retreat at The Castle, somewhat later in the calendar than usual, and after detecting the merest hint of a wicked glint in Nick's eye, I felt that our venerable Drum Major should be warned that the ancient cobble stones of the Castle Esplanade would not be as forgiving as the grass of Leith Links. Furthermore, it would be extremely embarrassing for all concerned for him to chase after a rolling mace, plaid flying, into the assembled crowd. On the other hand, he could possibly ignore the fact that the mace was no longer in his possession, and carry on marching. How silly would he look with his mace-less gauntlets in the air above his head, to signal the Right Wheel. Clearly it did not bear thinking about.

In the end, of course, the choice was his, and Nick being Nick, went for it. Big time. My heart was in my mouth as the ceremonial mace rose up in the air, the sun glinting off the polished silver. I swear to God that thing winked at me as it disappeared out of my peripheral vision, my head being held in place by my blowpipe. The other drum majors looked up, then looked at each other, aghast. I was beginning to assume that the mace had been sucked into a passing airliners engine, or even gone into orbit, the amount of time it was taking to come down. Maybe it had been an optical illusion, and Nick had fooled us all and still had the mace in his possession, just to picture our faces as we marched on behind him.

Agonisingly, down it came at last, spiralling like a sort of airborne drunken ice figure skater. Nick marched on about ten yards in front of me, ramrod straight, not even as much as a glance heavenward. The sound of the bands even slowed, as if playing on the wrong speed of a record player. It became like we were all wading through treacle, as one does in a bad dream. I suddenly became aware, and for no apparent reason, that this would be my last Edinburgh Castle experience, and that was truly sad. In fact, I realised with horror, that this was my last Fettes College Pipes and Drums experience full stop, but what a way to go. Forever remembered as the Pipe Major of Fettes the year their Drum Major dropped his mace.

Very slowly, Drum Major Urquhart's white gloved hands began to turn palm upwards. The crowds gasped in awe. It is difficult to describe, but do you understand me when I say you could have heard a pin drop? The other drum majors screwed their eyes tight shut, waiting for a massive 'clang' as silver met stone. But it never came. That mace settled down into Nick's gauntlets like a kitten going to sleep. They were, undoubtedly, two hearts beating as one, and I had dared to question their bond.

Every one of us, from time to time, has experienced an event in their lives that is perceived to be 'life changing'. Like your first kiss, or your first car crash. Or even the loss of a dearly departed limb. The thing is that we do not realise this at the time.

I was sitting on my upturned pipe box at the Fettes war memorial, waiting for Dad to pick me up, along with my worldly possessions, the last man of my year to leave our school. Allow me to explain. The annual shooting team trip to Bisley for the National Championships ran a week into the summer holidays, so by the time the 1st VIII - by now with me as captain - instructors, reserves, our rifles and the Sergeant Major headed off in the direction of London. Everyone else at school had already gone home. On the return journey we stopped off as usual at the Edinburgh Academy, and waved a passionate goodbye at our brothers in arms out of the back window of the coach. The coach moved off, stopped, then reversed back to the Academy gates. The extremely relaxed Academy guys as usual assuming that their rifles and kit had casually disembarked from the trunk of their own accord. Eventually back at Fettes the others had disappeared off to the train station or been picked up by punctual parents. Dad was late. However, I had one last, solemn, duty to perform, and in the stores the Sergeant Major was as impassive as ever.

"Glengarry, pipers, one."
"Plaid, one, water absorbing for the use of."
"Spats, two, complete with Tippex cleaning kit."
"Kilt, Royal Scots Hunting Stewart tartan, one."
"Doublet, Pipe Majors, one."
"Pipe Major's Banner, with Fettes College crest, one…"

In a daze, I handed back all my Band kit that I had been so proud to wear, as well as the army jumpers, boots and combat jackets along with my inverted four chevron Pipe Major's armband, that I had been wearing for the Bisley meet. I still wondered why on earth the Sergeant Major always wore his Argyll's tie over his jersey, and why, for goodness sake, did he tuck his jersey into his trousers? But as we looked at each other, no words needed to be said. I would have saluted him but I wasn't wearing a hat, so I turned and left. Then it hit me. I had now left school. What was in store for me, away from the trials and tribulations, the fun and the family that had been my life for five years at that school. I had given up my uniform, and with it my hard-earned rank. I was now officially a civilian, so to speak. I thought I might write a new tune. Perhaps 'Pipe Major Allan Jardine's Farewell to Edinburgh Castle' as a rousing March. Or how about 'Pipes and Drums No More' for a haunting Lament? A cracking wee Reel could be 'My Bonnie Wee Mace Flies Over the Ocean'.

Yes, life would indeed change all right, but would it be for better or worse? Where in the world would I end up? Would I buy an electric guitar, and become the depraved rock star I so aspired to? No more Pipes? Maybe there would finally be an end to backing up on to church walls, whilst playing at weddings, to prevent the back of my kilt blowing up embarrassingly in the wind, and so exposing The Secret to a gaggle of giggling and blushing bridesmaids. I smiled at the thought of never again having that itchy rash one gets on the back of one's legs, while travelling on a coach wearing a wet kilt, and smiled even more at the thought of no more of that infernal Highland Racket. Well, I could not have been more wrong about anything in my life.

There is a line from the song 'Hotel California' by The Eagles. You know the one, about being able to check out any time, but never being able to leave. Thus, it is so with The Pipes. Once a Piper, always a Piper. There were going to be a lot more shenanigans with these old things yet, and not just in Scotland.

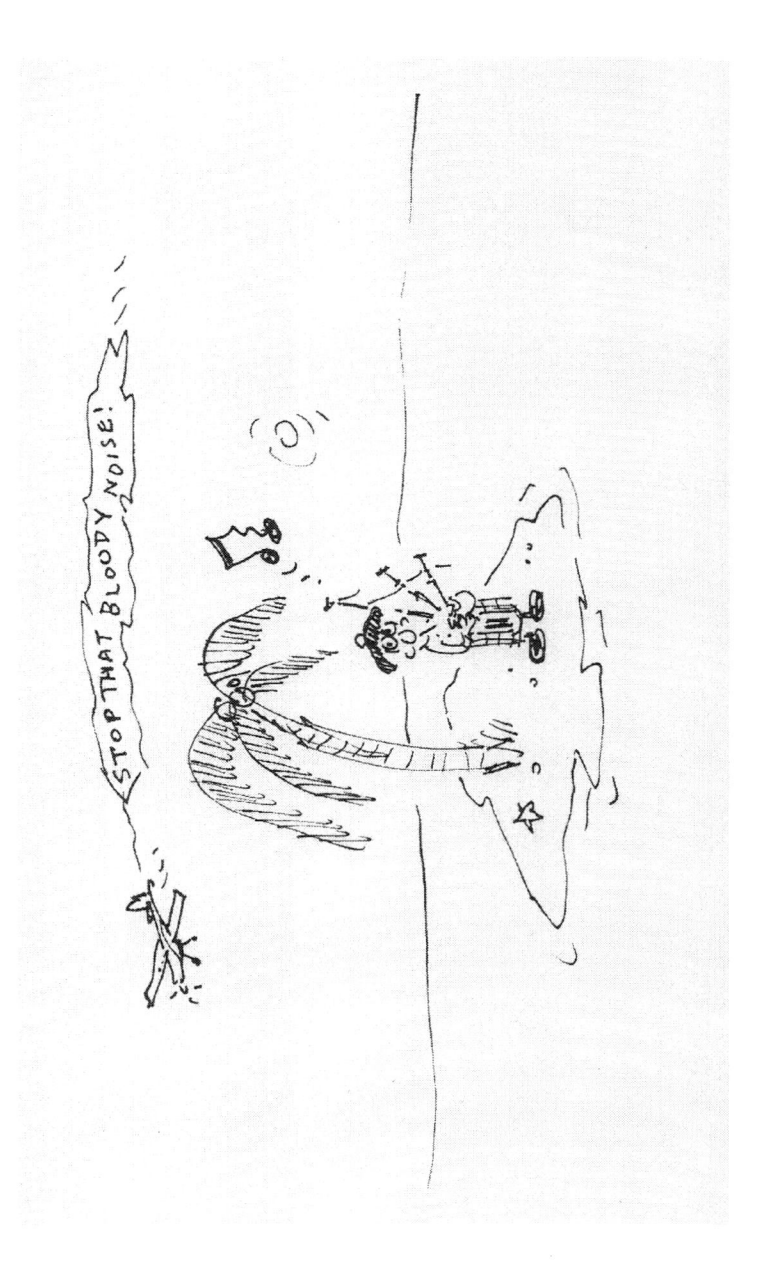

Chapter 9. No man is an island

East? West? Hame's best!

Robert Kirk

So, if I had wondered where in the world I would end up next, I had no idea it was to be at the other end of the world. I was to discover that Scotland is known for many things across the globe, and not merely the obvious ones such as Whisky, Tartan, and the hillwalker's friend, the horribly sweet Dundee Cake.

To be quite honest, we Scots have made quite an impact in the world, for a nation of a mere five and a bit million souls. Recently we even had a Wimbledon tennis champ, Sir Andy Murray. Individual sports again, but for a sporting pastime considered to be one for a warm and dry summer's afternoon, and considering our famously damp and cold climate, or 'dreich' as we call it, that's not bad, even if he did relocate to train in Florida.

But the people of our small country have influenced the world in other noticeable ways too. The list of ground breaking inventions and initiatives is too long to list here but as every schoolboy knows, television, telephones, electricity, steam engines, rubber tyres, penicillin, anaesthetic, adhesive stamps, the breach loading rifle, the raincoat, the vacuum flask, the Typhoid vaccine, hypnotism, Bovril, the U.S. Navy and even, amazingly, the Bank of England, are all products of the Scottish mind. And that's not to mention Adam Smith, the father of modern economics, or the musical imprint, ghastly or otherwise, of the Bay City Rollers. And who can forget that the first man on the moon was half Scottish, and that the first king of a joint England and Scotland was a Scottish king, by the way. Even the late Ugandan dictator Idi Amin liked to style himself as Scottish, even wearing an Argyll and Sutherland Highlanders glengarry, because he thought it was cool.

I found out from a young age that I am a direct descendant of a very famous Scotsman named Alexander Selkirk. This remarkable man was born in the village of Lower Largo, Fife, Scotland, in 1776 and desiring more out of his life than to join his fathers' business as the local cobbler, left to go to sea to seek adventure. After a few years of legalised pillaging of foreign vessels for their booty, or privateering as it was known, he returned to Largo but couldn't settle down. One last trip he thought, and ended up somewhere in the South Pacific, on a ship under the command of a Captain Straddling.

It was here, after his ship was shot up in an altercation with a Portuguese galleon, that he strongly advised his captain to put in to a friendly port for repairs. Tempers frayed, and the outcome was that young Alexander was unceremoniously dumped ashore at the nearest landmass, a small twelve-mile-long uninhabited strip of land around four hundred miles off the coast of Chile in South America.

Well, he thought, how bad can it be? There was fresh running water, an agreeable climate, enough material around for a makeshift shelter to await the next passing friendly ship, but that was just it. He could not signal to a passing vessel in case they were the unfriendly ones, so would have to make do till a ship bearing the appropriate flag actually put in to the small bay on this island where he was marooned. A few days then. Weeks at most.

So he settled down to wait, with nothing but the company of the wild goats that roam the cliff face, and a voodoo doll of Stradling he had fashioned for use as a coconut shy. Unfortunately for Alexander, it was to be a long four years and four months before salvation came, by which time he had become, according to his rescuer Captain Dampier, 'wilder than the original wearers of the goat skins that now adorned his body'. It is also logged that they could not at first understand what he was saying, assuming had forgotten how to speak, but that was probably more to do with an excitable Fife accent.

After he eventually made it back to civilisation nothing more might have been known of his adventure, but he became a celebrity due to the emergence at the time of free one sheet parchments, the forerunners of modern-day newspapers, distributed around the more glamourous coffee shops of the day, providing news of the Napoleonic wars and society gossip. His romantic tale of solitude soon found its way to a businessman by the name of Daniel Defoe, who promptly realised that here was a story worth telling properly, with a few embellishments of his own of course. Literacy among the people was becoming commonplace and Defoe's entrepreneurial senses saw his proposed story book as nothing more than a business venture as opposed to a radical new art form. It became the first ever published novel, and he called it *The Life and Adventures of Robinson Crusoe*.

And so it came to pass, in early 1982, that my good self and a small delegation from ours and Alexander's home village of Lower Largo, were off to visit his island on a sort of ambassadorial goodwill trip to deliver a plaque. And my pipes were going along too.

A trip such as this needed the usual preparations, so kilts were pressed and my silver medals were polished. My pipe box was going to be my hand luggage, because I feared for the pipes' safety in the hold. I had a clear out, abandoning such detritus as half full bottles of bag seasoning, old sheets of music manuscript, books of matches from rugby club bars, packets of chewing gum, used paper tissues, and a cocktail menu from the Craw's Nest Hotel in Anstruther, with someone's phone number scrawled on it. I left out my faithful practice chanter but kept such essentials as spare reeds, valves, needle and thread, adhesive tape and the odd safety pin. This all neatly made room for my Walkman, sunglasses, camera, the Berlitz guide to Spanish, and a bottle of Irn Bru.

I had decided to travel wearing my kilt, which seemed like a good idea at the time, but on arrival in Santiago, via Edinburgh, London, Madrid, Sao Paulo and Rio de Janeiro, the pleats at the back were in a dreadful state. A limousine was parked on the tarmac, so I glanced around to see if I could spot a famous actor or rock star in the huddle to disembark, carrying my box over my head, which seemed the best way to negotiate the scrum for the doorway. To my great surprise, on the sight of me in my dishevelled kilt, one sock around my ankle and sporran hanging lazily to one side, the driver of the long car was out and holding open the door and we were ushered in.

Well, talk about arriving on my first trip to foreign shores in style! It transpired that the founder of the Chilean Navy was a Scotsman, of all people, and the Navy and the Chilean military who ruled the country at that time, albeit with some bad press, were keen to offer us any curtesy during our stay. Indeed, the story of Alexander Selkirk was well known to them and as such, we were minor celebrities.

As we were led away to an informal reception, a nice lady informed us that our luggage would be taken away to be cleared through customs, but I insisted on accompanying my pipes just the same, and just as well I did. A set of dismembered bagpipes under an X-ray scanner looks most suspicious. Various tubes with metal rings here and there invited further investigation, but it was the bag that caused concern. There was something in it. It felt sort of test tube shaped. We shall, they said, have to cut open the bag to see what it is.

Oh no you won't! To the bemusement of the other travellers in the line, I frantically explained what the instrument was and how it worked, miming badly with flapping elbows, the action of playing and making the best approximation of the bagpipes whiney sound. The problem was a drone reed, normally fixed into the underside of the pipe, had become loose and was floating around in the coating of seasoning inside the bag. This happens from time to time and is merely replaced by a spare, until such time as one can be bothered to take the drones, blowpipe and chanter out of their stocks, and work it slowly out by the most available route.

My efforts seemed to do the trick, however, and my precious instrument was returned to me none the worse for its ordeal. Now, when I travel, I carry a photo of myself playing to show to uninitiated officials. The last time I flew into Germany they insisted on having their picture taken with the pipes on their shoulders, no doubt to show all their friends what an exciting job they have.

We arrived at the Juan Fernandez Islands by a small twin propeller engine plane, which landed on the only flat bit, on the south end of the now inhabited island called Isla Robinson Crusoe, the other two being called Isla Alejandro Selkirk and Isla Santa Clara. As it touched down we appeared to be hurtling toward the edge of a cliff, but the pilot made a sharp right turn just before the edge and we hurtled along the edge until we ground to a merciful standstill. No limos here, but a precarious climb down the cliff to a small boat which in turn took us around the coast to a bay where now sits a village of perhaps five hundred, who lead a pleasant existence, dropping their pots for crayfish on a Tuesday and picking them up on a Thursday, and drinking wine mixed with peach juice, in the sun, for the rest of the week.

The locals were there to greet us in force, so to mark the sense of occasion, and let's face it I hadn't brought them all this way for nothing, a wee tune was in order. My kilt by now was safely rolled up lengthways the proper way, not folded, to let the creases fall out and was in my suitcase, but this was the most informal of gatherings so jeans and a 1978 Scotland football shirt was the uniform order of the day.

Surprisingly, the pipes needed little fussing over, the dry and warm climate seemed to suit them well. Maybe, like tennis players, I thought I might relocate to Florida after this, and do us both a favour. Anyway, after some inquisitive looks from the natives, I was up and running and blasting out 'The Barren Rocks of Aden' as I marched along the jetty into the throng. The men were doing their best imitation of a Highland Fling, and the children were following me, trying to imitate the sound, giggling, with fingers in their ears. They had never seen such a sight.

A feast was prepared, of fish and crayfish straight out the sea, and I was shown the life size depiction of Alexander himself in his goat skins, gazing hopefully out to sea, painted on the wall of the school. He was their hero, and I, his noisy ancestor, had come among them.

After a few days wallowing in my celebrity, we sadly had to say farewell and I politely declined the Mayor's generous offer to marry any of the local girls I fancied and to settle down there, perhaps as a bagpipe teacher. I had grandly bequeathed my Scotland top to a local man who had expressed an interest in it from the moment we had arrived, and I was on my way home with some extraordinary memories. I shall return, one day.

Alexander Selkirk died of fever aboard ship at the age of forty-two, and was buried at sea off the coast of West Africa. I wonder if he knew that Captain Straddling's ship did indeed go on to founder of its wounds, and sink. The Captain himself and a handful of sailors were rescued by a Portuguese man o' war and ended up in prison, destined to labour in the salt mines of Peru for seven years. He would smile if he knew he had got by far the better deal in the end.

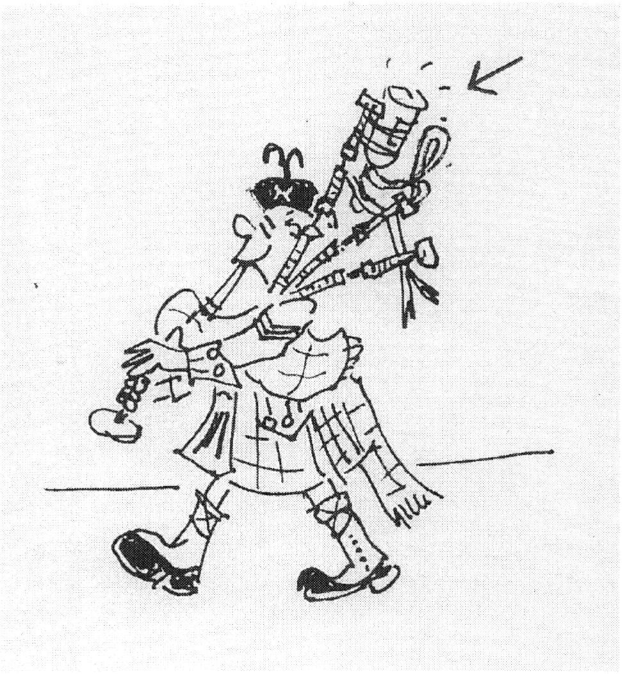

Chapter 10. The Water of Life

"Gentlemen, I have just met with the most wonderful adventure that ever befell a human being. As I was walking along The Grassmarket the street rose up and struck me in the face."

Lord Rockcliffe

The man was deliriously hysterical, and he covered the bartender with flecks of spit, as he jabbed a finger at in my direction and screamed, eyes rolling: "Get that Piper a Whisky!" Scotland's football team had just scored a goal. A very important goal apparently, necessitating the need for all the delirious and hysterical people in the pub to get their new best friend in The Land a whisky.

Because of the extreme link between nationality and the instrument, a piper's drink must be Scotch whisky. Let's face it, who ever heard of a man in a pub insisting on buying a piper a Campari and Sprite? Or toasting The Haggis with a Diet Coke. Perhaps, at midnight on the 31st of December, a glass of banana daiquiri or a rum baba would go down rather nicely. But I'm sorry, that's just wrong.

I read somewhere that more people in Italy, per head of population, drink whisky than in Scotland, and they are young, too. In Scotland these days, whisky is perceived to be an old man's drink, as well as a piper's drink. This is changing somewhat due to the growing popularity of whisky served in a cocktail amongst the younger and perhaps more 'drink aware' attitude of discerning drinkers. It is seen to be a better experience to savour a quality tipple over a longer period of time than the unhealthy straight shot. But we do live in a free society, and if your tipple of choice happens to be Absinth and cranberry juice, then so be it, but not for us Pipers though. Fortunately, I rather like whisky, and these days I sip mine mixed with Crabbies Green Ginger Wine, a Whisky Mac as it is called, for reasons unknown to me. But I digress. Maybe us huffers and puffers of Pipes build up an acquired taste for the stuff, having to quaff a *quaich* of the amber nectar at Burns Suppers from an early age. Whatever, if a man is wearing Scottish national dress, and playing traditional Scottish tunes on Scotland's national instrument, at a typically traditional Scottish event, then nothing else would be deemed appropriate.

So a brief history of *uisige beatha,* or Water of Life in Gaelic, seems to be called for here. This most popular spirit drink on the planet has origins that are as hazy as the origins of bagpipes, and for similar reasons. The art of distillation goes back to our learned friends in ancient Egypt and Greece, the process then being used mainly for medicines rather than pleasure, but you can see how there would be a natural overlap.

Later, as knowledge moved westward, the distillation of naturally fermenting drinks such as wine produced spirits such as brandy or sherry, a most welcome addition to the drinks' cabinet of the Scots, who up until now had relied on simple beer as refreshment. But the usual wars with France and Spain curtailed the import somewhat and people began to experiment with the native oats, which didn't work, but newly imported barley grown in the peat enriched soil and soft water of the Highlands, did.

I'm not going into the complexities of the actual processes here, or timelines, but someone found out that storing this new fire water for long enough in forlornly empty old sherry casks greatly enhanced the flavour and smoothness. It wasn't long before every farmer in the Highlands was producing the stuff, and as its popularity spread, the Government's ever-watching eye for the taxation coin became aroused. This drove the fledgling industry immediately underground, and it was even decided at one point to maybe ban it altogether, This was never going to work of course, and at one point half of all whisky being consumed by the wily Scots was illegal, with even church ministers hiding the precious liquid in coffins to baffle the dreaded 'excise men'.

In the end though, it made better business sense to avoid the stealth and the jail, cough up the duty, paid on the amount of malted barley used rather than the product itself, and reap the rewards of a ready-made market, a market ripe for export. King James IV developed a great affection for his *aqua vitae*, the Latin translation of Water of Life, so respectability became assured. It was even used as currency in the American War of Independence.

So I had piped our national team on to the field to do battle, and as usual the troops in the bar got well and truly fired up for the action, and as chief protagonist in the firing upping, the troops rewarded me in the usual fashion. They bought me drinks, namely whisky. But I did not mind this at all, and although I was gagging for a pint of lager, or maybe a nice cup of tea, I soldiered gamely on. At one point I decanted all my drams that I had stashed about, lying around on top of gaming machines and in various nooks and crannies, into a pint glass and found that I had an eye watering 3/4 of a pint. That's nearly a bottle for Christ's sake! It would, I reckoned, be extremely rude to waste any, but moderation must be observed.

Whisky, therefore, is the reason why none of the buttons on my Bonnie Prince Charlie jacket are the same. It is also the reason why there is a dent in the silver rim around my sporran (you'll hear that story later on) and why the sealskin tassels don't match. It is responsible for me losing that first kilt pin I was given all these years ago. Don't get me wrong, I am a man who is known to 'like a dram' as they say, but I can't help feeling The Pipes were what started it all off. Anyway, it is nice to have something to blame it on.

So now I come to another celebration of the Scots at play, complete with tartan, pipes and whisky. It is a most traditional of Scottish parties of live music, country dancing, Highland dancing and afore mentioned light refreshments, and is called a *Ceilidh*. A Gaelic word meaning a meeting, or gathering to exchange information. And what better way to do that than over some whisky, and see where that leads.

Now previously I have described the debauchery that is a Burns Supper. Imagine much the same at a *Ceilidh*, (pronounced 'Cay-lay') which was used originally to describe a gathering of people, but is now primarily a dance, so that rather than being safely slumped at a table, everyone is forced to jump about in the room, holding on to someone preferably of the opposite sex, at the same time attempting to all move in a big circle, backwards, in time to rather lively music. Think about it. This is hard enough to do when sober, let alone after many, er, refreshments. Here comes the analogy: imagine a herd of wildebeest, but in twos and on their hind legs, being chased by a lion. Then all of a sudden the ones at the front spot another lion up ahead, and frantically go into reverse, clattering into the ones at the rear who are still galloping away from the first lion. Yes, as you can imagine it's pandemonium, but here's the thing. Once one has consumed enough of the good stuff, who cares?

In my youth I had to yawn my way through these things, clutching my pipes tightly, and using them as an excuse as to why I was, truly unfortunately, not able to dance the Dashing White Sergeant with Big Agnes from the local family run fishmongers. I couldn't wait to finish my stint playing 'Mary Broons Troosers' or 'When I Was A Wenchin' Laddie' for the Highland dancers. I have to admit it was always a pleasure to watch the girl dancers whirring round like spinning tops, with their kilts flying out horizontally, and I had, guiltily maybe, long since discovered that the faster I played, the higher the kilts would rise. Their 'Secret' is that they wear pants. However, I was always glad to get home.

Now however I am older and back in the local village hall once again, but this time I sense things are just a little bit different. You can see what's coming here, can't you. After being forced, forced I tell you, to have a few large Whyte and Mackays after playing for the dancing girls at breakneck speed, I found myself thinking, why not join in? I mean, how hard can it be? What harm could possibly come of it? Heather, daughter of Big Agnes, was now sixteen years old, and if the faint but ever-present whiff of the family business was overlooked, she was turning out to be a right cracker, if slightly on the statuesque side for her age. A potential dancing partner for yours truly I reasoned, brimming with the confidence and arrogance that just the right amount of the Water of Life gives a young man. Did you know that in 18th century Edinburgh, several eminent physicians of the time were convinced that, with the correct daily dosage of The Water, a man could become immortal? Sorry, I digress again.

Back to the dance then. I was wearing my new gear of black evening jacket with silver buttons, a white dress shirt and a black bow tie, silk of course. I had a new made-to-measure Ancient Grant kilt and had sort of borrowed a magnificent silver rimmed sporran, one of Dad's best ones, without any intention of ever giving it back to him. A particularly handsome *Sgian Dubh* peeped out of the top of my right-hand white wool sock, and the leather soles of my patent leather dress shoes made a satisfying 'click' as I walked. All in all, I felt very James Bond. I stashed my pipes under a chair and swaggered over to Heather's family table, and this time I would not be asking for four large dressed haddock and half a dozen eggs please.

Young Heather required no persuading, and deftly had me in a headlock in an instant. She steered me onto the dance floor and we waited for the band to commence the 'walkthrough' of The Gay Gordons. The 'walkthrough' is where the dance is conducted at walking pace with no musical accompaniment, but with a member of the band giving instructions as to who goes where and at what point. This is necessary, due to the fact that as everyone gets so 'emotional', no one can remember the dance moves from the last *ceilidh* they were at. To this day I have no clue about what I'm supposed to be doing at these events.

After a few minutes of practice, the accordions and fiddles of the band struck up a rousing tune, and we were off. In different directions. Heather's hand grabbed me like a butchers' hook between the shoulder blades, and pressed my head to her bosom. Spinning around like this cannot be good for you, I was thinking, when the music changed abruptly and suddenly we were doing the backwards thing. I thought I was getting the hang of it when I missed the change to go forwards again, and dragged Heather back through the masses like a bowling ball through a stack of skittles. I have to admit to being a tad out of breath by the time we made our way back to the table in silence. Heather's heavily made up eyes bored through me like lasers from under her fringe, her hair being specially tinted and straightened for the occasion. It was time to head for the bar.

After a quick check on my old wood and silver friends in their box under the chair, I was decompressing at the bar with a Crawford's Five Star with just the same again of water, when there was a heavy tap on my shoulder. I turned round to come face to face with the most enormous pair of breasts I had ever seen, then I looked up. Oh, my good God, it was Big Agnes herself. The vast amount of perfume she was wearing not quite masking the smell of Pittenweem Harbour on market day. She knew I would have no excuse this year as I had already been on the floor, lying on top of her daughter at one point I admit, but on the dance floor nonetheless.

But, to prove a point about how too many whiskies impairs one's judgement, I thought hey, what the hell. Go for it. I downed my dram and slapped the glass on the bar. This time the dance was the Eightsome Reel. There was a rumour that a sixty-foursome reel was performed after the wedding of Mary, Queen of Scots, but the record of a one hundred and twenty- eightsome reel, if myth is to be believed, was performed for an enthusiastic General visiting the Gordon Highlanders in Aden Barracks in 1946, roping in the cooks, the Military Police, three German prisoners of war, and the guests and waiters from an Italian restaurant in the town to make up the numbers*.

The essence of the dance is that four sets of couples line up facing each other, then when the music starts everyone starts interlocking arms and spinning each other round, and swapping partners, while at the same time prancing about like a young deer. I am aware that there is supposed to be a pattern here, but on this occasion I had absolutely no idea what I was doing. I attempted to compensate by increasing my prancing to almost comical levels, but soon found myself amongst a completely different set of couples than the ones I started with. Big Agnes had disappeared somewhere, and bizarrely at one point I found I was being spun most violently, as if in an act of revenge, by the aura that was the lovely Heather. Maybe it was just as well the fair Heather and I didn't hit it off that night. These days she runs the family business, and is known, although not to her face, as Even Bigger Heather.

After the music stopped I realised, looking around, that it was over and I could stop all the prancing and mincing stuff and giddily made my way back to the bar. It appeared they had run out of Crawford's so I moved on to Highland Park instead, ruminating that before I did any of this dancing malarkey again, I would take lessons, or buy a manual or something. The irony struck me that if I had taken to the floor in my younger, sober days, perhaps I would have remembered the moves, and then when completely trousered, could have danced on automatic pilot.

I wondered if other cultures have the same sort of problems. Morris dancing while totally plastered on Oxfordshire mead could have dangerous consequences and the Chilean tango after slightly too much of the Pisco Sour seriously so. Maybe, in the United States, line dancing whilst slightly sparkled on Kentucky bourbon could be fun. I decided I might go and find out, and I would take my pipes with me, just in case.

*See the excellent memoir *The General Danced at Dawn* by George Macdonald Fraser for details.

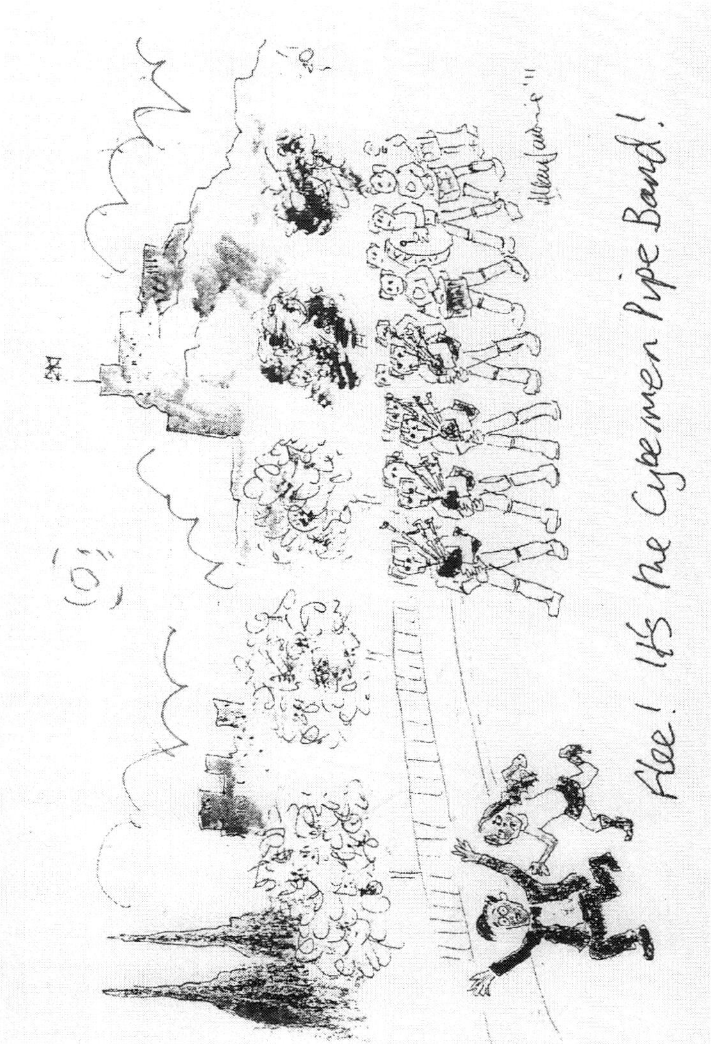
Flee! It's the Cybermen Pipe Band!

Chapter 11. The Black Death

"We shall not cease from exploration, and the end of our exploring will be to arrive where we started, and know the place for the first time."

T. S. Eliot

"The world is your lobster."

Arthur Daley

I know I said I was off to the States, but this story really starts in Iceland of all places. Having been a student in Dundee for a few years, I was now back living in Edinburgh and was working in advertising, and I reckoned I was well overdue for a holiday. I went to visit my mate Gavin, who was by now also in Edinburgh managing a hotel, to see what sort of mischief we could get up to.

Gav and I had been getting up to all sorts of mischief since we were six years old. When we first met, I remember that I was wearing a cowboy outfit, and he was wearing the dress uniform of a Guardsman. I was most impressed. Not a great deal had changed, except that now, when I popped in to his work one Sunday evening, I was wearing the uniform of an Officer Cadet in the Territorial Army, and Gav was done up in a bow tie and kilt, to welcome yet another coach party of old people from Birmingham or wherever, keen to explore the beauty and history of the country.

I threw my Tam O' Shanter bonnet, with the badge of 2/52 Lowland Division (Royal Scots) on the bar, and took a seat as Gavin went through his usual routine about what time breakfast was, what direction the Castle lay, (look out of a window, madam) and yes indeed madam we do stock English gin (Gordon's) and yes sir we do indeed supply English tonic for the accompaniment (Schweppes), to the audible relief of all present. I was sorely tempted to point out to the plump lady with prominent teeth and enormous glasses beside me to carefully check the spelling on the tonic bottle label. Oh yes madam, 'Sch...' is, in fact German, but I did not want to have Gavin cope with all the fainting and mass hysteria, so I kept quiet.

My pipes were rarely out of their box these days. I did not play in a band, entered no competitions, and apart from the odd wedding, rugby game, Stockbridge Duck Race and, of course, Hogmanay piss up, things were relatively peaceful and free of The Racket. So we decided they should come with us on our adventure. After all we were away over New Year, and as everyone knows, a Scotsman becomes, well, more Scottish when away from home, so our kilts were coming as well. As I have propositioned before, what harm could it do?

Well let's just see exactly what harm it can do. The destination chosen was Florida, and more specifically, Fort Lauderdale, as we had read that this town was party central. It is the famed choice for American students to take the debauched Spring Break, so if the place was debauched enough for these guys, it was going to be debauched enough for us. Gavin phoned a few days later with the news of a cheap, flight only deal he had secured, via Iceland, but only for a refuelling stop, but one which would give us a little time to see the sights. Apparently, the noble people of Iceland have taken to flying into Glasgow to do their Christmas shopping, partly because they have few shops of their own, but mainly because it is much cheaper. Unless that is you want buy a big jumper with all the colours of the rainbow knitted into it, and obviously everyone already has one of those.

So finally the kilts were rolled carefully lengthways, the only way to transport a kilt as it preserves the pleats, rucksacks were packed, silver was polished and we were off to the airport at last. The Sunshine State here we come. As well as doubling as hand luggage on these trips my pipe box is also handy when waiting in a busy departure lounge, as I can prop it up on its end and use it as a seat.

The flight, predictably, was full of Icelanders who all seemed to know each other, and they kept swapping seats to catch up on things of an Ice nature. It turns out that the population of the entire country is the same as Edinburgh, and Edinburgh can be pretty small sometimes I'll admit. The best way to bump into some you haven't seen for a while here is to hit the city centre at Christmas, pick a spot and stand still. I guarantee you that within five minutes some old girlfriend, or a former work colleague whose name you can't quite remember will come strolling past. And this is what was happening here, only 20,000 feet above the North Atlantic. We had been told at immigration that the runway would be in darkness by the time we had refuelled, and because of a snowstorm it was deemed too dangerous to take off until morning. We were to be put up in a hotel with dinner thrown in, so great, we thought. Let's do Iceland.

Once it leaked out on the plane that I had a set of pipes with me, lots of offers to visit houses or meet at bars were scribbled onto scraps of paper, by these extremely welcoming people. After a bite to eat in the hotel, and a small gulp of a bottle of Glayva that Gav had bought at Duty Free, we hit the town, armed with our scraps of paper. I've no idea what the licencing laws are now, but trust me, in mid-1980s Iceland duty-free beer was banned, but spirits were not. I would have thought it would be the other way around but there it was. That was why there were so many cases of Tennent's Lager coming off the baggage carousel at Reykjavik International Airport.

We chose to visit a bar that we had been told about with a folk group playing, and sure enough, there were our friends from the plane. Our arrival had been predicted and anticipated and the cries immediately went up for a performance. I was still trying to get my pipes out of the box and assembled as I was pushed towards the stage. After a frantic tune up, I was straight back into the groove. The fingers never lose it but I was soon out of puff due to lack of practice. My run through of a few quick reels, and Scotland the Brave to finish, which everyone always recognises, had them up dancing. Job done though, and to wild cheering I made my way back to the bar, not to the usual pile of whisky, but to a hooch popular in Iceland by the name of Black Death Vodka.

This, it turns out, is very aptly named. It even comes in a coffin shaped box, with a skull and crossbones as a label. Slash, legendary guitarist of Guns n' Roses and Velvet Revolver is apparently a fan, so that speaks for itself. This stuff is hallucinogenic. The closest I can get to describing the effect is that it feels like being able to breath under water. Gravity is suddenly no longer an issue, and everyone looks like an extra in the film 'Finding Nemo'. It's like having a party on the sea bed. We ended up at someone's house drinking till the early hours and got a taxi back to the hotel. My only memory is of playing the Irish jig 'Paddy's Leather Breeches' down the radio to the taxi driver's wife, before being told off by the hotel concierge for waking everyone up.

The next morning I was understandably hungover, but we were on holiday. My mouth tasted like the inside of a Turkish bus driver's glove, but it wasn't so much the rough feelings as the acute raging paranoia. I kept thinking I was about to pass out. I had to resist the urge to yell out obscenities at complete strangers, or to stop hyperventilating. Once aboard the plane again it was worse. Apart from motion sickness severe claustrophobia kicked in almost immediately. I was so desperately thirsty but could not hold down any water. If someone had suggested that the amputation of my right leg would make it all go away, I would have gone for it. Much to Gavin's concern, I spent the entire eight-hour flight in the toilet.

At Orlando airport, they pushed my off the flight in a wheelchair, dribbling, with my pipe box across my knees. It had been cold in Scotland, and even colder in Iceland when we had left, so now Gavin was wheeling me along wearing my heavy jacket over his own heavy jacket in 90-degree heat. I was almost in tears as I refused to get on the train to the baggage terminal, as I could bear no more motion. In the end I made it, and now Gavin had a rucksack over each shoulder as well. A minibus trip from hell now lay ahead to a hotel Gavin had booked by simply pressing a photo of it on a screen. The driver had to stop twice on the way. He was not happy about it, but as Gav explained I was either sick on the road or sick inside his vehicle. And then finally, mercifully, a bed, a dark air-conditioned room, and oblivion as Gav gaily tripped out the room to find some cans of beer to go with his Glayva, and a hire car. Welcome to Florida.

I recovered quickly though, and pretty soon we were cruising South down the A1A in our tiny but very reasonably priced car. At once we could see something was fundamentally wrong on the image front, and at the first opportunity pulled into a car rental to upgrade to a Chrysler LeBaron convertible. Man, this was much more like it, even if it did mean we were being sunburnt down one side of our faces. All the motels on the Fort Lauderdale beach strip looked pretty much the same, but one stood out. The Jolly Roger, with its bar built like the prow of a ship, and the staff in bikinis, bandanas and eye patches - seemed to draw us in. Base camp established.

That evening we got talking to two wise guys from Chicago, who were here till Christmas, and seemed to know the lie of the land. It was agreed that we would 'party' with them the following night and as they had found out we were Scottish, and had confirmed their theory that all Scotsmen wore kilts and played bagpipes, the pipes at least should make a guest appearance. Steve and John had another theory that our novelty value would get us all introduced to girls, and we had absolutely no problem with that. So the next night, with a hearty slap of fresh sunburn and newly purchased Hawaiian shirts, a sticker bearing the legend 'Welcome to Fort Liquordale Beach' stuck on my pipe box, we indulged in a small dram of Glayva in the room before heading out for some action. We left the kilts out at this point in case there were rules.

Now we were just two shy lads from Fife, so it was much to our astonishment when the action started almost immediately. Steve and John introduced themselves to a table full of girls in a bar, then introduced us with an added: "...and this dude plays bagpipes!" It had been my intention to do the rock star thing and drink Jack Daniels, but no, the piper/whisky thing had obviously crossed The Pond, possibly with the many Scots early settlers, and a large Johnny Walker Red Label was thrust into my hand. I was going to have to give them a tune now, but was not relishing the thought of having to play in every bar we went to. Not much of a holiday, I was thinking.

It was once observed that nobody looks cool in the back, as opposed to the front, of a convertible car, but now, a few hours later we were tearing down the strip, with me sat on the boot of Steve's orange Mustang whilst playing 'Scotland the Brave'. How cool is that? This, it has to be said, is much more fun than dreary old village Burns Suppers, and people were cheering and waving, and one girl even bared her breasts for good measure. Outstanding! We had also built up quite an entourage by now, and it was decided that I should pipe us into an 'All U Can Eat' seafood bar. No problem there, for a man who has led ten bands out of Edinburgh Castle. After a slight hiccup when my drones got tangled in some fairy lights strung around the door frame, we were in and began grabbing handfuls of prawns, our plates over flowing so that most of it was on the floor.

After we were turfed out of there, it was on to a gentleman's club or 'titty bar' as John called it. Shortly after being asked to leave by some very imposing bouncers I realised with horror as the car sped off that I had left my pipes behind. This is the one and only time I have ever let my pipes out of my sight, and will remain so. I was so distraught that rather than wait till the next turn off, Steve decided to bounce the car across the central reservation and head back straight away.

This was pretty much the tone for the rest of the time our Chicago friends were around. We bade a fond farewell to Steve and John on Christmas Eve, and spent Christmas Day on the beach, like you do. Things were fairly relaxed after that, apart from a frantic, hastily organised emergency trip down to the Florida Keys for a couple of days. I had simply assumed that the beautiful blonde heiress with the chunky bodyguard and the Corvette was over the age of twenty-one if she was being served drink at the bar. Also, I was informed in hushed tones that her dad was someone big in the Miami underworld.

Hogmanay was the usual mess you might expect from two young Scots abroad, and kilted up. Proudly I would like to say we did not disappoint, and we had made many friends. We had one last drive around town before heading back north to Orlando, hopefully having the other side of our faces burnt to even things up, and then home for a rest. It had been hard work having fun. We stopped off in some obscure wee bar way off the strip for a cold beer before hitting the I 95 Freeway, only to be greeted by the bartender shouting: "Hey, it's the Scottish dude with the bagpipes! You still have five shots of whisky in the till from New Year's!" Oh dear.

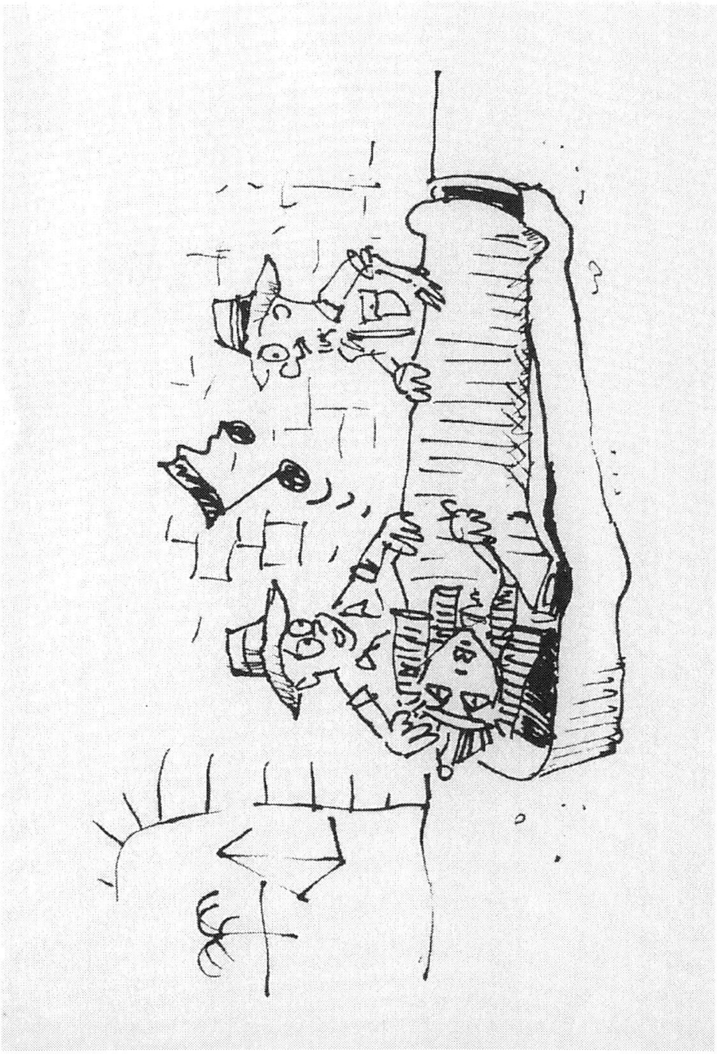

Chapter 12. Cherry tomatoes

*"And in the end it is not the years in your life that count,
it is the life in your years."*

Abraham Lincoln

It was very bizarre, the way I ended up teaching the pipes in Taiwan. In fact, 'bizarre' is a most accurate description of the entire trip. The word also sums up rather neatly the people and their culture, the landscape, the traffic, the food, lifestyle, education system, rules of etiquette, use of technology, treatment of foreigners, politics, and laws. While we're at it, 'bizarre' would also describe their attitudes to family, authority, learning, manners, socialising, religion, money, and entertainment. Not forgetting music, art, traditions, celebrations, marriage, travel, public transport, and death. If I've missed anything out I apologise, but you get the general idea.

Now please don't get me wrong, I loved that country. I will always remember the friendliness and helpfulness of the Taiwanese people, and occasionally I will cast a nostalgic eye over the many photographs that I took, of the many friends that I made there. The visions of a family of five travelling through suicidal traffic perched on one tiny scooter always makes me smile. Dad drives, Mum rides pillion, eldest child hangs on to Mum, then any younger ones, and finally the baby balances on the handlebars. I remember fondly the way everyone hangs their wet laundry off the electric cables slung between the houses, and how they shout a greeting as you pass. How I'll never forget the children, bless them, who on a daily basis would, with huge smiles, offer me local 'delicacies' such as dried snake eyes, or my favourite, aesthetically anyway, 'deep fried whole sparrow on a stick'. They knew full well that I knew that they knew that I was unable to refuse their kind offers on the grounds of their 'giving and receiving' customs, the rascals.

It all started one summer back in the early nineties, when the pub I was managing back in Fife, The Victoria in St. Andrews, was closed for refurbishment, and I was at a loose end. What, you may ask, has this got to do with taking something so uniquely Scottish and so wonderfully clamorous to the other side of the world? Well, that week, just for something to do, for fun if you like, I took a short course in Teaching English as a Foreign Language at St. Andrews University. Can you see where this is going? I had no real desire to actually teach anywhere, but if I did, perhaps Prague, or maybe Monaco. Tuscany during late summer would certainly suit.

I had to walk past a notice board near where the class was held, with all sorts of foreign job offers on it, which I largely ignored, but this day one lonely little scrap of paper beckoned my eye. As I drew closer it was as if it suddenly jumped off the wall, grabbed me forcefully by the lapels and stuck itself right in my face. And so began another of those life changing moments I spoke of earlier. Once more The Pipes were to be back in my life like a hard slap across the jaw. "Teacher of English wanted for students aged five to seventeen. Pei Yuan High School, Changhua, Taiwan, Republic of China. Salary, free accommodation and meals. Must be able to play and teach Scottish Bagpipes." It might as well have added: "Must have the name Allan Thomas Jardine".

"No." I groaned inwardly to myself. I had never been enamoured of the Far East because of the food; my idea of a seafood platter being a battered haddock. But it was no use. I got home that day and agonised over what to do. At that period in my life I had no real commitments, and my on/off relationship with my girlfriend was in 'off' mode. Sensing that the planets were aligning, the next day I had popped into a local travel agent and asked the two plump but extremely tanned young girls with hair scraped back into buns, if they had any brochures. "Thailand?" One of them heaved herself out of her chair and moved toward a stand containing many magazines with images of sandy beaches and turquoise sea. "Er, no, Taiwan, Republic of China." I'm sure the couple who were entering as I was leaving were wondering what on earth had put these girls into such hysterics. It would appear that no one went on holiday to Taiwan.

Eventually, I actually had to drive to the main library in Edinburgh to research what I might be letting myself in for. People might still assume that the 'Made in Taiwan' label applies to cheap plastic toys, but not anymore. These days the computer chips you take for granted are made there, and it's a fair bet that your mountain bike frame is also 'Made in Taiwan'. Little is known about this small island country lying a few hundred miles off Hong Kong, and they have been quietly and busily becoming extremely wealthy under everyone's noses for years.

There is no British Consulate or American Embassy there and very few countries in the world recognise it at all. This is because mainland China regards Taiwan as a rogue state of the Motherland, colonised by Chinese Nationalists after the war with the Communists in 1949. China has stated that if Taiwan ever formally declares its independence, then China will invade. Not a good scenario all round, so other countries do their political business with Beijing, and little Taiwan plods away, working hard, becoming rich, and all the while, learning. During the Olympic Games it is referred to as Chinese Taipei. Taipei being the capital, literally just to keep the peace.

Right, that's the boring stuff out of the way, but it is important that you know. I found out that kids over there start learning English at three years old. Three years old! Our kids are barely learning English at three years old! And get ready for this. The typical school working day starts at 7 am and ends at 9 pm. What is that all about? Oh, and Saturdays 7 am until lunchtime. Sunday is known as a 'holiday' and thank God for that. Ominously, I could find no reference to the length of a typical school term, or indeed any mention whatsoever about musical instrument tuition, let alone the size of a typical school Pipe Band. But, I reckoned, if they wanted me to teach Pipes to three-year-olds, I was going to have take some miniature practice chanters with me for miniature hands. And what about the bagpipes proper, for goodness sake? Maybe, when I arrived there, I could look up a telephone directory, to find 'Ping Lu McFadden, Traditional Highland Bagpipe Maker (none of yer plastic rubbish) Cut Down Sets for Toddlers A Speciality'.

As you can probably tell by now, I had decided to cry 'Geronimo!' and jump. Like buying that last, but important present on Christmas Eve in the cold, dark, lashing rain, it simply had to be done. As I mentioned, I am not even a fan of Chinese food over here, which I can promise you is very much westernised, let alone typical school dinner scoff over there. No more mince and tatties for a while.

I studied the address on the crumpled scrap of paper, pulled out a copy of my C.V., looked nostalgically at a photograph of my younger self standing proud in my Pipe Major's uniform, and went to my sock drawer to check if my passport was still valid. Some choices in life are made because fate has provided an opportunity, and you know I love saying it, but how hard could it be? I was by now an accomplished guitar player as well, and just wished it was the opportunity to teach guitar at a school in the Bahamas.

The first rather alarming shock, and there were to be many, on finding the train station to take me from the capital, Taipei, to my new home was that the signs were all in Chinese characters, of which there are over 2000 compared to our twenty-six. I did not know which was southbound or northbound or anybound for that matter. Think about this for a minute. If one is in, say, Germany, a travelling fellow can look up the word for 'bagpipe' in a dictionary, and find the translation: '*doodlesac*'. Easy peasy, as the letters of the Roman alphabet apply to both languages. We can even have a reasonably good bash at pronouncing it correctly. But this gobbledygook neon signage I could neither translate, decipher, nor pronounce. I certainly could not look anything up.

Before total panic set in I remembered the name of the town that I'm headed for is pronounced 'Changhua' so I could at least buy a ticket. I asked a youth wearing a business suit and a New York Yankees baseball cap: "ticket office?" to which came the astonishing reply: "On your left, as you go between the bookstore and the McDonald's. It's approximately 300 yards. You can't miss it. The first-class booths are the red ones, second class blue, and third class are a sort of mustard colour. I wouldn't go third class though if I were you, there's no air conditioning so the whole carriage reeks of sweat." Ah, yes indeed, thank you. Learning at three, eh?

Well, this might be easier than I thought, as I watched the strange countryside fly by out of the packed train window. I was hoping it was not far as my fellow passengers were becoming increasingly irritated as at every station I would enquire "Changhua?" to a chorus of: "No Changhua!" I knew how to pronounce the word, but did not know what it looked like on a station sign. Mercifully, soon there was a deafening chorus of: "Yes Changhua!"

My next problem was to get myself, rucksack and pipe box through the crowded train before it moved off. Being the good sorts that they are, the other travellers helped by pushing me through, and indeed off the train onto the platform, followed with a thud by my pipe box and the rest of my kit. I wasn't even up off the ground when I was mobbed by twenty or so men, shouting and tugging and pointing feverishly at the taxi rank. I broke free, and assured the cab drivers that before I went anywhere else, I was going to find the nearest bar and de-stress.

Now this was the next shock to the system. There are no bars in Taiwan, at least not in the way we might think of them. There are hotels and restaurants which sell alcohol of course, and cafes which they call 'tea houses', and in the larger cities they might even have a themed Irish pub, but in this town of three million people, there are five bars. I know because I trudged the streets to find them. On my last week there I bumped into a young man just arrived from Perth, Scotland, of all places, who asked me in a hoarse and desperate voice: "Where are all the bars?" I will never forget the look on his face as I bequeathed him my worn town map, with five very important crosses marked on it.

After some time wandering the streets, I ended up sat on my upended pipe box, knackered, grumpy, and sweating profusely on a pavement outside a supermarket, with a carry out of cans bearing the legend, in English thank God, of 'Taiwan Beer', the only type the shop stocked. Incidentally I did discover that you can buy your cigarettes in a bakery, the public toilets are a hole in the ground, and the hairdressers double up as brothels, so be careful what you ask for in there. I was not due at the school till the next day, so I booked into a guest house and spent the evening in a theatre, having bought a ticket merely to use its adequate bar facilities – although the background music was truly dreadful - and take stock of the situation. Tomorrow was going to be a big day.

To answer the question you have been asking, the reason these people wanted a bagpipe teacher, was that there had been a school trip to Scotland the summer before. They found that here indeed was something wild and strange to them. Of course, it was an absolutely awesome noise, but obviously hard to learn, and therein lies the key. Boy, do these people like to learn.

I'm not joking when I say their eight-year-olds are doing maths that our sixteen-year-olds can't handle. To fill in any gaps in the curriculum they study useful stuff like basic medical aid, and explore the workings of the internal combustion engine, in case their scooters break down. This is because in all that traffic, neither an ambulance nor a mechanic is going to get to you in a fix. At the end of a class many Taiwanese pupils will approach the teacher's podium, and ask for some of the finer points of the lecture to be clarified, so that they are satisfied in their own minds that they have understood everything. Our lot simply bolt out the door the second the bell rings, leaving a flutter of pieces of paper, discarded books, and the odd shoe.

So, then, here I was in the cavernous concrete dining room of the school, sticking out like a penguin at a polar bear's wedding. The headmaster was beaming as he said a few words, presumably of wisdom, then horror: he was asking me to introduce myself to the 600 or so pupils. The air of curiosity and expectancy was reaching fever pitch in the acute silence of the room as I moved to the proffered lectern, and wrote 'Mr. Allan Jardine' on the blackboard. I was as nervous as the time of my first piping competition, but just like all those years ago, I rose to the occasion, adjusted my Royal Scots tie, and soldiered on.

"Today?" I enquired of them as I wrote '1st September' on the board. Yes, they unanimously agreed. "Today is the first day..." I continued cautiously, "of the new school term." Another resounding "Yes!" I was on a roll now. "Yesterday," I spoke slowly and precisely as I had been taught, and wrote 31 August, "Holidays!" There was a low murmur and then silence. A line of sweat began to dribble down my back. "Ah, er, vacation?" Not quite as enthusiastic this time, they chorused despondently: "School."

Uh, oh, what's going wrong here? Well it turned out that the poor sods had all been sent to cram schools in their holidays, although the word 'holiday' is a slight contradiction in terms. I had not unpacked yet, and sure as Hell wasn't going to until I found out if I was expected to teach from 7 a.m. to 9 p.m., Saturdays till lunchtime, fifty-two weeks of the year. Mercifully my timetable showed twenty-two hours a week, and I even had a Wednesday off as well as the 'holiday' on Sunday. Also, you will never guess, but my evening piping classes were a Tuesday and a Thursday, just like when I was at school. Knowing The Pipes like I did, there was probably a military decree somewhere, or statute of some kind, proclaiming that all classes worldwide would be on those two days, to commemorate something or other. I bet that at The Crimea some young piper won a Victoria Cross for playing all day Tuesday until he was knocked unconscious by a canon ball, lay in the mud all the next day, then woke up on Thursday and started giving it some more skreetchy stuff to scare the Russians all over again. Honestly, it would not surprise me.

Actually, while I'm on a rant, I'm amazed there is no tune specifically to be played while a band remove or return their instruments to their boxes. There are military ones for wake up in the morning, flag raising, lunch, end of day, mess call, officers mess change for dinner, officers mess pre dinner drinks, dinner, after dinner drinks, vomit into fireplace, and lights out amongst other things. Maybe I should write one and call it 'Tae A Box'.

Moving on, and I was eagerly anticipating giving my first Piping Lesson after a few successful language ones. I strolled into the classroom expertly twirling my faithful old chanter between my fingers, and was greeted by a selection of ages, all boys, cheerfully clutching the terrible plastic practice chanters and crap tutor books I mentioned earlier, bought from tourist tat shops in Edinburgh. My own chanter, with its broodingly handsome dark mahogany finish, deep yellowed ivory band around the middle, and the grooves at the tip where my teeth had worn away the wood after much toil over many years, drew a ripple of appreciation and approval. Here indeed was an Esteemed Teacher, a Noble Leader. A Great One. I had gained great 'face' it would appear.

Without further ado, I beckoned to a big lad with a huge toothy smile and a number one haircut, and played a basic scale. He took the hint and played the scale back to me, toiling with a furrowed brow as he did so. Not very encouraging I thought, but then what must I have been like when I started? His attempts at a few grace notes were woeful, not his fault though, he simply needed more guidance and, of course, practice. The next two were not much better, and I could see that the future of this particular pipe band lay well into the, er, future.

The next wee chap was different. He actually started to play 'Amazing Grace', not very well admittedly, but all the movements were there, and the look of concentration on his face was intense. There was an enormous amount of spittle bubbling around the mouthpiece, and there was something decidedly odd about the way his fingers lay on his chanter, which worried me in a strange way. I could feel that he had been waiting for this moment for some time, ever since he gazed upon the fingers of the busker in Edinburgh last summer, fascinated by the speed and the dexterity, terrified, yet in awe, of the awful unholy noise. Now was his chance to show what he had achieved from a crap tutor book, on a plastic chanter, to perform in front of a real, live, Master of the Discipline.

The others keenly watched me watching him.

He was their best. Their Champion. What would be the reaction of The Teacher? He ground to a halt at the end of the tune, and looked up. Not expectantly, but more apologetically. The nature of the noble people of Taiwan is to strive towards perfection, and this humble kid knew he still had some work to do, but also that he had given it his best shot under the circumstances.

My reaction was to immediately walk out the door.

I hurried back to my quarters, and returned to the classroom with The Pipes. Much was the interest as I assembled the drones, wet the leather valve in the blowpipe with my tongue, made sure the reed in the business end was secure, did some other pre-flight checks, and inflated the bag. My thoughts went back to the day when I first saw these pipes after Pipey had restored them, I think because of the looks on the faces of these wee future pipers. This, at the end of the day, was what it was all about.

After the pre requisite tune up, and a quick burst of 'Jock Wilson's Ball' just to show off, I beckoned to the kid with the excess saliva and the weird hand notation. And yes, you guessed it, I had the pipes plastered all over him in an instant. After us both struggling for a minute to get the blowpipe in his mouth and his hands on the chanter without the drones falling off his shoulder, it suddenly hit me. His hands were the wrong way round. Bagpipes are played with the left hand above the right, with the drones on the left shoulder, with no exceptions. The reason for this is to maintain symmetry within a band. I am aware of the existence of 'left-handed' sets these days, but I'm not sure how this would look, or even be allowed, in a Pipe Band. I gently put the pipes down on a desk, and picked up my practice chanter. Now it hit him as well. Emotions were running high in the room as he picked up his chanter and, with trembling fingers, copied my hands and struggled to contemplate the fact that he would basically have to start all over again, with his hands the 'right' way round. All that effort was for nothing. The tears began to well up in the wee man's eyes.

By now the others could see it as well, and they felt for him. Their Best Man had tripped at the last hurdle, leaving the rest of the field to gallop on past him, after having been so far ahead. He had landed on the '99' square of the snakes and ladders of life, and had gone back to square one. It was quite literally a crying shame, as the tears started to flow - they're an emotional lot - and before it got me going too, I decided to act.

I don't care if there is a military law, dictum, directive, or indeed a covenant handed down from the MacCrimmons of Skye, this kid would continue to play just the way he did. Fair enough he would be a little lopsided stood outside a church, in the rain. Or instead of smashing a light bulb in the roof of a function room, with his bass drone, he might take out a window instead, but that would just be too bad. I knew what it was like to learn this bastard of an instrument, and no one on my watch was going to have to learn it a second time over.

Crisis averted then, and we all had a laugh when, at the end of the class, I was presented with one the many 'delicacies' I was to receive as a thank you for teaching them that day. This one was in the form of a frog, that has had a stick rammed up its arse while still alive, and then been dunked, spread eagled, into a pot of boiling oil. Its poor wee features forever petrified in a mixture of agony, humiliation, and bewilderment. When I bit into it, it sort of 'popped', like when one bites into a cherry tomato. It was truly disgusting.

Lovel has a problem Houston, he can't get his pipes to work....

Chapter 13. A stitch in time

"Music… in time of care or sorrow, will keep a fountain of joy alive in you."

Dietrich Bonhoeffer

My flight out of Taiwan left on Christmas Day, and because of the nature of the time difference, it would be a rather convenient Boxing Day by the time I touched down in Scotland. Even more conveniently there were just a few days to go till Hogmanay, and I can think of no better day than that to become reacquainted with the decadence and debauchery of the West, after the rigours and decorum of the East.

I had been very homesick over there, not so much for Scotland, but rather the whole Western Hemisphere. It was the little things I was looking forward to, like using a knife and fork, and to eat my meals in peace and quiet. You cannot imagine the noise of 600 hungry children using washable metal chopsticks, clicking wildly away in their stainless-steel bowls, in a cavernous concrete dining hall. And all this whilst excitingly discussing the American baseball league, or advanced calculus. I wanted to go back to handing over bank notes with one hand instead of two, which I was always forgetting to do, and so would cause offence as paper is sacred to these people. I wanted marmalade and toasted bread. And fried potatoes, cheese, Lorne sausage, steak pie and black tea rather than green tea. All the unhealthy stuff for that matter. And milk from a cow, not a soya bean. I wanted to be sarcastic again and tell rude jokes, in a bar. I also wanted to push my pipe box under the bed, and let it collect some dust for a while. I would miss the kids, though.

The last connecting flight was a British Caledonian one from Amsterdam, having flown via Bangkok with China Air, and while there I phoned my mate Gavin to pick me up at Edinburgh Airport. On the plane I almost wept when I heard the soft Scottish accent of the stewardess giving the safety lecture, and like the Pope, resolved to kiss the tarmac on landing. In the end, I didn't kiss the tarmac on landing at all as the rain was bouncing off it like bullets, and anyway I was much more interested in getting in to town for a serious pub crawl that would rival the Crusades in carnage. "What do you want first?" Gav ventured cheerfully, as he greeted me in the arrival hall. "A bean and tattie pie or a pint of lager?" It was a close call but the pint won, so we abandoned the car somewhere and headed for the Old Town. I was gasping for that beer, in its straight glass, so much I was almost breaking into a trot. Then, at last, I was sat at the bar of the famous Jinglin' Geordie pub, and I can still taste that pint today. This had been the last pub I had been in before I had left on my adventure. Full circle, I was home.

As usual, the jungle drum telegraph system that works so particularly well in Edinburgh was swiftly at work, and the sister pub to 'Geordies' soon had me booked in to perform on the 31st. The Antiquary on St. Stephens Street, in the delightfully bohemian area that is Stockbridge, has always been one of my favourite hostelries, and although I had my cottage in Fife at this point, I could stay at Gavin's till after New Year. Obviously, I had all my gear and pipes with me, so what could possibly, possibly I say again, ever go wrong?

What indeed you may say with a smile, I hope. This last chapter will cover the importance of checking equipment and the area where the performance will take place. Not that long ago, performing at some bankers work retirement do in the Edinburgh Hard Rock Café I forgot my own drills, and caused much merriment amongst the diners, and consternation to the management, as I smashed a spotlight in the roof with my bass drone, whilst piping in –I kid you not- a haggis burger. Always check the height of the restaurant ceiling. In the Crusoe Hotel in Largo the ceiling is so low that I have to play leaning backwards, and with my knees bent, and that is not a pretty sight. Ungainly, and certainly not military.

Whilst on the subject of checking, make sure your route to the 'top table' is hazard free. I remember being caught out at a Burns Supper in my youth where everyone stood up in the two lines of tables to clap me in. As it was a small room, I had resolved on this particular occasion to march straight up the middle, but when the chairs were pushed back, I had no room to squeeze through. The chap carrying the haggis behind me took the initiative and went to go around the outside, but we faced exactly the same problems trying to fight our way between the chairs and the walls of the function room. By this time, I had repeated 'A Man's A Man For A' That' three times so we admitted defeat and stopped where we were.

The haggis was duly passed up the line to the 'Chieftain' and my dram of whisky passed down. One does learn from one's experience. Quite amusing looking back, but a tad embarrassing at the time. Here's another one. Churches quite often have more than one exit. Ensure that the door you saw the bride enter, is the same one that the happy couple will leave by.

The title of this chapter is, rather cleverly if I may say, entitled: 'A stitch in time…'

Never leave home without a sewing/repair kit in your box. I refer to mine as my survival kit. Tactical repairs to instrument, gear, and self when out in the field are part of the job specification. A buckle here or strap there if not repaired immediately can cause much disruption to the occasion or function in question, not to mention the extreme embarrassment to the piper, or the audience even, and maybe even exposing The Secret.

There is a little flap of leather known as the valve, at the bag end of the blowpipe, which opens as the piper blows air in, then closes to stop it all rushing back out again. This had broken off just before I was about to entertain the masses at the Scottish Tartans Society annual dinner one year in Comrie, Perthshire. I had to improvise by cutting a piece from the leather insole ripped out of my brogue shoe, and fashioning a new one with scissors, which surprisingly lasted for years until it finally made its way to the great J & R Glen shop in the sky. This did not cause a problem this time, as I had wisely made sure there was a spare in the box. Carry spares of absolutely everything.

But back to my story about Hogmanay at The Antiquary, and a good example of planning and preparation for the performing piper. I had not really unpacked my stuff, and most of my clothes were a might whiffy anyway. In Taiwan, I had to wash my clothes by hand and so had just given up during the last week. Maybe the last two weeks. Whatever, I borrowed a couple of T-shirts from Gav and enjoyed the next few days lazing about gorging myself on sadly missed scotch pies, white puddings, bridies, fish suppers, oatcakes, pate, mince, mashed potatoes, and tattie scones, all covered in lashings of brown sauce and mustard. This I washed down with tea with the divine, heaven sent luxury of added milk and sugar.

Then the Great Day arrived, and the old pipes were out of their box once again, as indeed I would be later on that evening. A quick polish and then I cast my scrupulous and well-trained eye - hey, I was an Instructor now - over the reeds, bag to drone connections, blowpipe valve and other bits and bobs necessary for the tartan octopus to make the Big Din. As with the reply when asked the perennial question of whether anything was worn under the kilt: no, everything was in perfect working order. Good as new in fact.

We decided it was high time to be heading out, so it was relatively easy to pack my kilt and its accessories as they were kept in a separate part of my luggage to keep them away from the smelly stuff. At an event of such a magnitude of over indulgence, I would change nearer The Bells so as to minimise damage due to the inevitable beer spills, cigarette burns, and odd and unexplained stains such as lipstick or creosote. Tuning up would be done in the pub cellar as Gav, understandably, did not wish to alarm his neighbours.

A good few hearty pints followed, with the ladies and gentleman who give The Antiquary their patronage. I concentrated on reading the time on my watch through my pint tumbler mid slurp, and decided it was time to get organised. Armed with the keys to the cellar and my holdall of kit, I retrieved my pipes from behind the bar and headed purposefully off. I was wondering idly how many New Year's Eves I had piped at, but could not seem to be able to deduct the age I started, seven, from my present age, possibly due to the extra whiskies that had appeared from kind benefactors and so gave up. The pipes were sounding just perfect and looking good, so now it was time to get me looking good as well.

White dress shirt on, kilt on and adjusted so as to hang just so. Next my dented silver topped sporran, that used to belong to Dad, strapped on at the correct height. Now my bow tie, Royal Scots cufflinks and The Dagger removed from the sporran and all three applied to the assembly. Then the waistcoat and jacket, with any stray hairs and fluff being removed with a ball of masking tape I keep in the pocket. Also in the pocket, surprisingly, looked like what appeared to be a menu from a Taiwanese restaurant I must have nicked as a souvenir. Oh well. I put my jacket on and looked fondly at the inscription on the silver medal on the lapel: 1972. A long time ago now. I gave it a blast of beery breath and a tender wee buff up with the cuff of my jacket, and it sparkled like a diamond in its appreciation.

Finally, I reached into the holdall for my – Oh my good God! Socks! Where the hell are my socks! I stared into the holdall willing my long cream woollen socks to appear, but there was just my shoes looking reproachfully up at me.

Damn! What was the time? Nearly quarter to midnight. Damn, Damn! Gavin had given me a pair of horrible Homer Simpson nylon ankle socks he had received as an unwanted Christmas present, and now I stared at them in utter horror and disbelief. I clapped my hand to my forehead as I knew what had happened instantly. When I was packing back in Taiwan, I removed my passport and other important documents from my sock drawer, then tipped the entire drawer contents into a plastic bag and then into the rucksack, and of course my kilt socks were in there, not with the rest of my kilt attire which had been hanging neatly on a hanger in the wardrobe.

What a disaster. I would be the laughing stock of the pub if I strode out wearing patent leather dancing brogues with the long laces that tie up the leg, over yellow and blue Homer Simpson ankle socks. No, it would simply never do. My watch said 11.45. I stripped off and changed back into my jeans and trainers, and belted out passed all the punters, who exchanged bemused glances. I ran as if the Devil himself were after me. I ran past groups of singing revellers, and swerved around couples snogging in the middle of the pavement. Like the fugitive running from the cop in an American TV show, I chanced my luck and ran through moving traffic. There was too much at stake here to worry about being run over and killed. Onwards and up the hill towards Gavin's flat, I ran like a man possessed, or in this case not possessed, of a pair of socks. With trembling hands, and heaving chest I struggled with my keys and then I was in the stairwell of the tenement. Needless to say, Gav lived on the top floor, but I was already taking the stairs three at a time. I glanced at my watch. 11.53.

I sort of triple jumped first into the flat, then my room, and then head first into my rucksack. Kilt socks located and I was off again into the night. Downhill this time at least, which was actually my downfall, as I slipped on the icy cobbles, banged my knee and scraped my face along a pavement that felt like it was made of broken glass. Actually, it was broken glass, from a dropped bottle of celebration juice of some sort. The time was 11.55.

Up and away once more, limping slightly from the dodgy knee, but around the last corner and there it was. The soft welcoming glow emanating from 'The 'Tic' and the sound of merriment within. 11.57.

Sorry, I know the suspense is killing you, but I must explain at this point why the chapter title: 'A stitch in time…' is so fiendishly, if I may say, clever. The stitch referred to is nothing to do with sewing like you thought, but everything to do with the stitch in my side as I crashed through the swaying throng like a bowling ball on steroids. And the time? 11.58.

Back in the cellar, a pretty young red-haired barmaid in a Scotland rugby top and a tartan cowboy hat kindly attended to the blood dripping from the cuts on my face with some serviettes, and dabbed away with antiseptic from the kitchen first aid kit that stung like hell. She blushed heavily as she discovered her reward was to inadvertently learn The Secret of What Is Worn Under the Kilt as I breathlessly stripped off yet again, and more or less jumped in to my kilt gear all at once, like putting on a spacesuit. 11.59.

Eager to help, another barmaid had burst in wearing a pink T-shirt proclaiming 'I Was A Bad Girl Hogmanay '93/94' as well as the tartan cowboy hat, and was busy trying to put on my bow tie as I was trying to tie my shoe laces. In different circumstances it would have been an interesting ménage a trois. 11.59 and 30 seconds.

The bar manager stuck his head around the cellar door to anxiously check the progress. "It's twenty seconds to go, Allan." I was well aware of the time. "Just hold the bloody door open!" I bellowed at him over the girls' heads.

"Ten, nine, eight…" the crowded pub screamed in euphoric unison.

So then, yet another scrape, literarlly, gotten into because all these years ago my father decided it would be a good idea to have a piper in the family. It would even have been better if he had just told me that The Pipes were to be thrust upon me, rather than insult me by asking me if I wanted to play them first, and then dumping me with them anyway. But I have to ask myself the question; what if it had been the tuba? Or even a church organ? Quite inconvenient for travelling, and where would I keep my hipflask?

"Seven, six, five..." The Antiquary seemed about to explode with excitement.

Another thing about Pipes, is that everyone seems impressed that I can play them. Oddly, for the National Instrument of Scotland, there are very few of us who practice the art, and in a way that makes me proud. Proud of my instrument and of my country. OK so they're a bit noisy, but it's our noise, and that's why we love them. It's the same with the kilt. Sure, it is uncomfortable and impractical, but when wearing it, one cannot help but stand a little taller, and walk with a swing in one's step. Ask any man who has worn one.

"Four, three..."

It was that by now familiar slow-motion thing again. I brushed aside the girls' attentions and lunged for my pipes, my leather soles sliding wildly on the stone flags of the cellar, like a dog trying to sprint off a polished kitchen floor. I was on the move toward the door. Sometimes I wonder why I don't just sing in a choir, or play cello in a string quartet. I'm sure they don't have as much stress making their music as I seem to. The drones were thrown over the shoulder, my fingers fell onto the oh so familiar holes in the chanter, and the blowpipe, sensing the urgency of the situation, found its own way into my mouth. Slowly, the bag began to inflate.

"Two..."

It suddenly occurred to me that I had never played while totally out of breath before.

"One."

The pub erupted in a frenzy as the familiar, rousing, strains of 'Scotland the Brave' blasted its way into the bar. My breathing was forced into a steady rhythm, which meant that to compensate my heart rate was galloping like a racehorse. I was half way through the tune when I had to give in and stop, but no one seemed to notice, or even care for that matter. The moment had passed, but the moment had been good. Then it was hugs, handshakes and whisky all round, and Gavin asked who on earth had beaten me up in the cellar. My face was stinging, and I must have looked a right mess. I noticed that blood from the cut in my knee had dribbled on to the god-forsaken sock, and on further inspection the buttons on my waistcoat were out of synch so that there was a spare hole at the top, and a spare button at the bottom. Also, I had not tightened my sock garters properly so The Dagger had slipped down and was now nestling around my ankle, and my bow tie strap was under one wing of my shirt collar and over the other, but do you know what? I just didn't care. I just burst out laughing.

I retreated from the melee back to the tranquillity of the cellar, to return my pipes to their faithful box, the initials ATJ faded now, but still visible. I dismantled them carefully as I have done on so many occasions, and laid them gently down in the soft green velvet lining, fraying at the edges these days. My dear old pipes had never let me down. Before I closed the lid, I noticed it was about time to buy some new silk chords that join the three drones. One was being held together with a safety pin, and that's not right.

I thought of my dad, and how proud he was of his Piper. I thought of Pipe Major Barron, and Mr. Percival and Edinburgh Castle and beach bars in Florida, and the grim drizzle on a November day outside a Registry Office, and smiled. I wondered how the kids in Taiwan would get along with any new piping instructor. Don't laugh, but maybe I could find a job as an instructor here, now that I had experience. We need more people to play these things.

Seriously, there should be a Piper available for every single bar in Scotland at Hogmanay, because there is nothing, nothing in the world that stirs up the passion in Scottish people like the sound of the pipes. It is why they have been so effective in battle. It is why I had to run for these socks. It is why we stand outside churches, in the rain, playing

'Mairi's Wedding' because it will give just that extra touch to an already perfect day for the wedding party. It is pride and passion. That is why we love the pipes. It is why, and dare I say it, that The Pipes and everything associated with them, are in fact, cool, and I love them.

Did I ever tell you the story of how I got the dent in my sporran? It was falling down the outside of Aberdour Castle, but that's a story which will have to wait for volume two. And what is really worn under the kilt? Sorry, it's a Secret.

Catriona always enjoyed a spot of 'extreme piping'.

Epilogue

*"Some say that Scotland is God's country.
That's bollocks, it's our country!"*

Sir Billy Connolly

I am outside waiting to pipe in the guests at the Edinburgh College of Art annual ceilidh, and I have just worked out that I have been playing now for fifty-one years. It is February, it is starting to snow, and I am still suffering for my art. Soon, it will be time for my gloves to come off, and for my fingers to start seizing up in the cold, so that I can play no more.

My thoughts drift back those years, to when I first started and I could hardly hold a set of pipes let alone play them. I have no children, but I wonder if I had, would I send little Thomas off to piping lessons every Tuesday and Thursday? He would not like it, but I would explain to him how he would be the most popular man in the room on Hogmanay, I would tell him of the great camaraderie within a Pipe Band, and of the thrill of playing in one. I would tell him how all the girls would want to dance with him at parties, and that he would drink for free anywhere in the USA.

I would tell him of far off lands, where even there the power of the instrument is revered and admired, and so therefore, would he himself be revered and admired. I would repeat the old adage that the two greatest gifts that God can bestow upon man are to be born Scottish and a Piper. When he is older, I might let him into The Secret, of what is worn under the kilt.

So then, to force the child as I was, or not force the child. Would I not let him chose his own musical destiny, the same way that he must chose his own destiny in life? Well, I would buy him a chanter for his seventh birthday, see if he takes to it. But he'll also get a guitar.

Allan T. Jardine March 2021
Dedicated to the memory of Captain T. Allan Jardine 1921–1986

Appendix 1.

Police record

"I don't have a problem with drugs. I have a problem with the police."

Keith Richards

The following is a list, and quite possibly not all, of the police 'incidents' that have occurred as a result of my good self being associated with the most excellent company of the bagpipe kind. I would like it to be made clear that I have never been charged for any of these so called 'misdemeanours', and regard them as preposterous infringements of my God given liberty to perform as a Piper. So there.

Scottish Tartans Society, Comrie, Perthshire. Caution. Noise late at night.

Burns Supper, Morningside, Edinburgh. Caution. Noise late at night, holding up traffic in the middle of the road.

Hogmanay, Stockbridge, Edinburgh. Caution. Noise judged to be breach of the peace, drunk and disorderly, cheek to police officer.

Customs, Boston. Detained. Suspected illegal earnings to be made whilst busking or other pursuits with pipes.

Train journey Philadelphia to Tampa. Escorted off train after playing in buffet car in the middle of the night, due to protracted celebrations to mark retirement of Ted the bartender, as well as the release of Julian from jail.

Customs, Chile, South America. Detained. Suspected illegal drugs in pipe bag. The bastards just about cut it open!

Customs, Taiwan, Republic of China. Detained. I had been given a leaving gift that was a cigarette lighter, unfortunately in the shape of a revolver.

Customs, Edinburgh. Detained. *Sgian Dubh* causes security alert. The Dagger eventually travels to Frankfurt in a diplomatic pouch in the cockpit, instead of down my sock.

Customs, Frankfurt, Germany. Detained returning to Edinburgh for the same reason. These days it would have to be left behind altogether.

Hogmanay, Colinton, Edinburgh. Caution. Accusing an English policeman of making racist remarks, even if possibly quite true, with comparisons to certain animals as regards the sound of Scotland's National Instrument.

Hogmanay. Somewhere in Edinburgh. Arrested. Accused of exposing The Secret to passers-by. Cleared, and let out the car after real perpetrator is caught elsewhere.

Ceilidh, Aberdour Castle, Fife. Stern talking to. Wilful damage to a listed building while attempting to climb it, and falling down the side of it. More damage was done to my knees and the silver rim on my sporran.

Easter Road Cemetery, Edinburgh. Moved on. Reported as loitering with intent while waiting for people attending a funeral to leave so I could have a practice. Neighbours won't allow me to play in my flat.

Children's Gala Procession, Largo, Fife. Threatened with arrest for remonstrating with a police officer, for in all probable likelihood doing the crossword over the radio, while I was being water bombed by kids up on the viaduct.

Pear Tree Bar, Edinburgh. Arrested. Accused of encouraging the brawl that broke out as Scotland beat England at rugby to win the Grand Slam by playing 'Scotland the Brave'. Police later said they only arrested me to diffuse the situation and prevent a full-scale riot. I can, of course, see their point.

Appendix 2.

Countries played

"There's no place like home."
                               Dorothy Gale

England	London
	Manchester
	Catterick Barracks, Yorkshire. (Playing the personal pipes of Pipe Major Dippie, with the band of the Black Watch).
France	Paris
	Plessis-Robinson
Germany	Hamburg
	Frankfurt
	Munich
	Bremen
Norway	Kongsberg
Iceland	Reykjavik
Spain	Madrid
Holland	Amsterdam
Taiwan	Taipei
	Taichung
	Changhua
Chile	Santiago
	Juan Fernandez Islands

United States	Philadelphia, Pennsylvania
	Penn State University, Pennsylvania
	Boston, Massachusetts
	Washington D.C.
	Chicago, Illinois
	Aurora (we're not worthy), Illinois
	Biloxi, Mississippi
	JFK Airport, New York City
	New Orleans, Louisiana
	Miami, Florida
	Fort Lauderdale, Florida
	Dunedin, Florida
	Treasure Island, Florida
	Clearwater, Florida
	Tampa, Florida
	Daytona Beach, Florida
	Key West, Florida
Republic of Korea	Seoul
Scotland	Everywhere